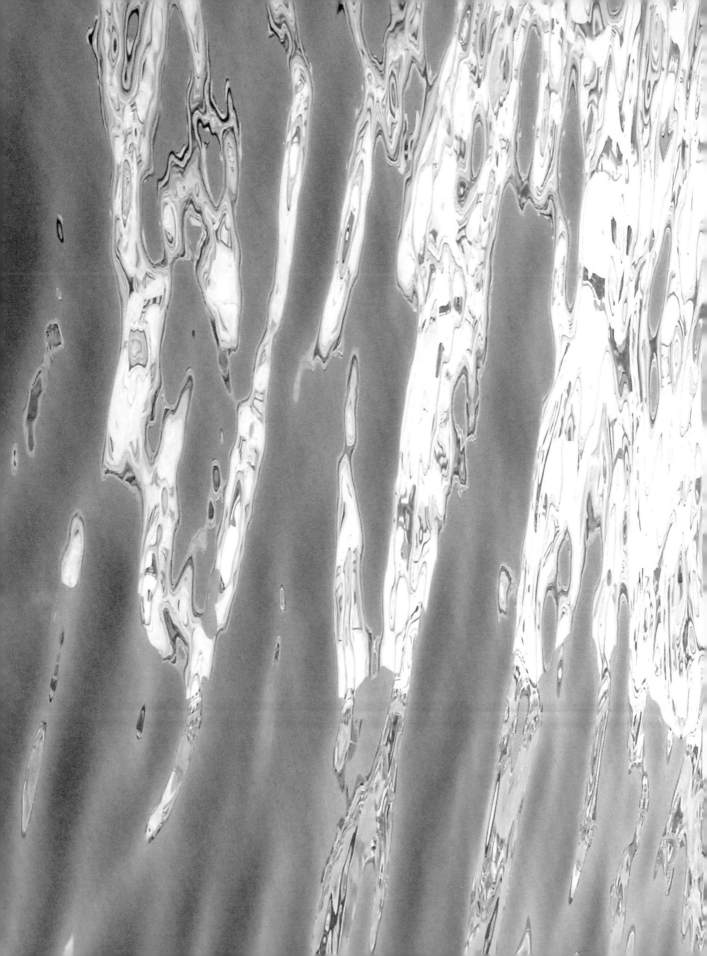

IN AT THE DEEP END

COOKING FISH
VENICE TO TOKYO

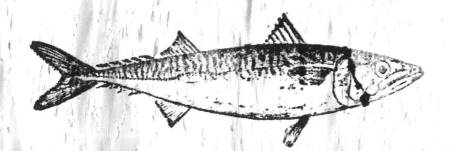

JAKE TILSON

Quadrille
PUBLISHING

Dedicated to my family with love

FROM LAGOON, TO SEA, TO OCEAN

VENETIAN LAGOON

NORTH SEA

NORTH ATLANTIC OCEAN

PACIFIC OCEAN

EXPLORING SEAFOOD KITCHENS

My seafood journey has been a shared experience over several years across lagoons, seas and oceans. Always at my side helping me along have been my wife, Jeff (Jennifer Lee) and our daughter, Hannah, this book is as much theirs as it is mine. Our culinary travels wouldn't have been possible without the generosity of family and friends and their glorious kitchens. Thank you to my parents, Joe and Jos, for many memorable Venetian adventures in our new family home in Dorsoduro. In Sweden, Andrew and Viktoria Cowie shared seafood delights with us, and took us to markets, restaurants and shops, day or night. Thank you too for letting your cat Tolstij appear in the book. Thank you Mary Lee for letting me loose in my favourite Scottish kitchen, and also for joining in on our wonderful coastal tours. In New York several excursions were aided by the extreme kindness of Peter, Linda and Ronnie Goodrich Mills, who gave over their kitchen for a bit of collaborative seafood cooking. In Australia, James and Jacqui Erskine's generosity knew no bounds – they lent us two stunning kitchens 1,200 miles apart in Sydney and Port Douglas, in which to wreak culinary havoc.

FIRST PUBLISHED IN 2011 BY
Quadrille Publishing Limited
Alhambra House
27–31 Charing Cross Road
London WC2H 0LS

EDITORIAL DIRECTOR Jane O'Shea
ART DIRECTOR Helen Lewis
PROJECT EDITOR Simon Davis
DESIGNER Jake Tilson
PRODUCTION DIRECTOR Vincent Smith
PRODUCTION CONTROLLER Leonie Kellman

EDITED TEXT, DESIGN AND LAYOUT © Jake Tilson 2011
AUDIO GUIDE PODCAST PUBLISHED BY Atlas ©&℗Atlas 2011

Cataloguing-in-Publication Data: a catalogue record for this book is available from the British Library.

ISBN 978 184400 975 6

Printed and bound in China

OTHER BOOKS BY JAKE TILSON
A Tale of 12 Kitchens, 2006
3 Found Fonts, 2003
The Terminator Line, 1991
Breakfast Special, 1987
Excavator-Barcelona-Excavator, 1986
Exposure, 1980
8 Views of Paris, 1980
Light and Dark, 1979

'... *fish is one of the great untapped areas of exploration, for curiosity, and for the delight of the cook and her family and friends.*'

JANE GRIGSON
Jane Grigson's Fish Book

FOR AS LONG AS I CAN REMEMBER I HAVE ALWAYS BEEN SCARED OF FISH.

AS A FAMILY COOK I'VE LEFT ENTIRE CATEGORIES OF COOKING UNEXPLORED FOR DECADES, PARTICULARLY SEAFOOD. MYSTERIOUS ICE-LADEN MARKET STALLS ARE SIDESTEPPED, INTIMIDATING SEAFOOD RECIPES LEFT SAFELY ON THE SHELF. I WONDER IF THERE ARE DEEPER REASONS FOR MY UNWILLINGNESS TO COOK UP SOME FISH FOR SUPPER OTHER THAN CULINARY NEGLECT? WHEN I DISCOVER WHY I'M SCARED OF FISH I DECIDE TO PUT THINGS RIGHT.

 # SPLASH

Far out at sea alone in the water, my body exposed beneath to the unseen icy green I'm caught away from the boat. The sky darkens, my chin clear of the frothy waves I manage to spit out a salty mouthful and gasp in some cold evening air. Thin, swirling currents of marbled water freeze around me like the sudden contours on a map. That's how I remember it – a fragile pattern fixed to my thoughts like hoarfrost. From that moment of extreme lucidity what followed next remains out of focus and submerged. Below the delicate and intricate traces petrified onto the surface something was moving, dark and large. It took six seconds to pass underneath my bare feet and then rose slowly to break the surface next to the boat before its intended arc turned towards me. Its thick, scarred fin looked like an exclamation mark cutting through the water.

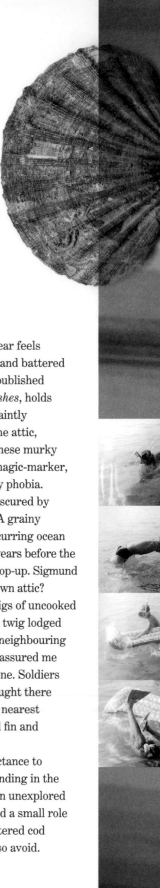

That was forty years ago but I can still taste the salt and blood in my mouth. The fear feels both real and present. Standing in our dusty attic, crammed with cardboard boxes and battered suitcases, I notice some faded childhood books, large azure volumes about oceans published by Time Life. The first book seems harmless enough but the title of the second, *Fishes*, holds something between its blue-board covers I'd thought forgotten. Flicking through faintly remembered pages I reach the section on sharks, and there they are – lurking in the attic, waiting for me, resurfacing and ready to devour me yet again. As a child I copied these murky photographs of man-eating sea monsters. Drawing hundreds of them in pencil or magic-marker, a boy obsessed. The book I'm holding contains the originals, the perpetrators of my phobia. Side-on views depicting various shark species, an action shot of a dolphin attack obscured by blood-filled water. The final page opens the gaping, skeletal jaws of a great white. A grainy black-and-white photo of the same jaws I'd seen before they consume me in my recurring ocean nightmare. So this is where my fear of fish and sharks stems from – a book – seven years before the celluloid version in 1975 would cement it in forever. And here I am getting a phobia top-up. Sigmund Freud would be proud of me. Where better to stow away your phobias than in your own attic?

A teenage encounter with an experimental sandwich prepared with several sprigs of uncooked thyme rounded off my fish phobia nicely. The thyme was rather woody, a bone-like twig lodged in my throat as I hurriedly ate it. My parents drove me to our family doctor in the neighbouring village, through a blustering storm. After a quick examination our doctor kindly reassured me that the claustrophobic feeling in my sore throat was just scarring, the twig had gone. Soldiers talk of there being a single bullet with your name on it. Since then I have often thought there was one fish bone out there with my name engraved on it, itching to take me to the nearest casualty department. So I keep to the shallows, watching out for a cinematic dorsal fin and avoiding seemingly innocent fish fillets on menus.

My sudden realisation of these fishy phobias goes some way to explain my reluctance to cook seafood over the years. A chef wouldn't get past basic training without a grounding in the fundamentals of fish, but as a domestic cook entire categories of cooking can remain unexplored for decades. Although I come from a family obsessed with cooking, sadly fish played a small role on our childhood shopping lists. The local fish and chip shop, Geales, served up battered cod fillets, always a safe fish choice for children, any bones were fairly easy to see and so avoid.

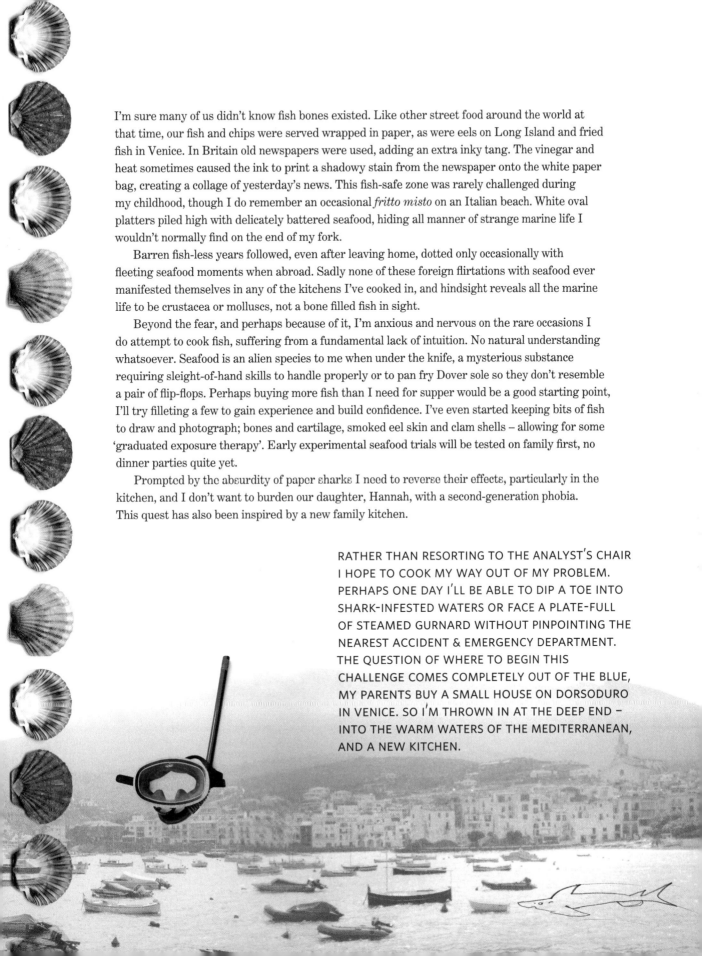

I'm sure many of us didn't know fish bones existed. Like other street food around the world at that time, our fish and chips were served wrapped in paper, as were eels on Long Island and fried fish in Venice. In Britain old newspapers were used, adding an extra inky tang. The vinegar and heat sometimes caused the ink to print a shadowy stain from the newspaper onto the white paper bag, creating a collage of yesterday's news. This fish-safe zone was rarely challenged during my childhood, though I do remember an occasional *fritto misto* on an Italian beach. White oval platters piled high with delicately battered seafood, hiding all manner of strange marine life I wouldn't normally find on the end of my fork.

Barren fish-less years followed, even after leaving home, dotted only occasionally with fleeting seafood moments when abroad. Sadly none of these foreign flirtations with seafood ever manifested themselves in any of the kitchens I've cooked in, and hindsight reveals all the marine life to be crustacea or molluscs, not a bone filled fish in sight.

Beyond the fear, and perhaps because of it, I'm anxious and nervous on the rare occasions I do attempt to cook fish, suffering from a fundamental lack of intuition. No natural understanding whatsoever. Seafood is an alien species to me when under the knife, a mysterious substance requiring sleight-of-hand skills to handle properly or to pan fry Dover sole so they don't resemble a pair of flip-flops. Perhaps buying more fish than I need for supper would be a good starting point, I'll try filleting a few to gain experience and build confidence. I've even started keeping bits of fish to draw and photograph; bones and cartilage, smoked eel skin and clam shells – allowing for some 'graduated exposure therapy'. Early experimental seafood trials will be tested on family first, no dinner parties quite yet.

Prompted by the absurdity of paper sharks I need to reverse their effects, particularly in the kitchen, and I don't want to burden our daughter, Hannah, with a second-generation phobia. This quest has also been inspired by a new family kitchen.

RATHER THAN RESORTING TO THE ANALYST'S CHAIR I HOPE TO COOK MY WAY OUT OF MY PROBLEM. PERHAPS ONE DAY I'LL BE ABLE TO DIP A TOE INTO SHARK-INFESTED WATERS OR FACE A PLATE-FULL OF STEAMED GURNARD WITHOUT PINPOINTING THE NEAREST ACCIDENT & EMERGENCY DEPARTMENT. THE QUESTION OF WHERE TO BEGIN THIS CHALLENGE COMES COMPLETELY OUT OF THE BLUE, MY PARENTS BUY A SMALL HOUSE ON DORSODURO IN VENICE. SO I'M THROWN IN AT THE DEEP END – INTO THE WARM WATERS OF THE MEDITERRANEAN, AND A NEW KITCHEN.

BACALA FOR BREAKFAST

DORSODURO, VENICE

A QUIET NEIGHBOURHOOD IN A SHIMMERING SEAFOOD CITY WHOSE SALTY CANALS HIDE SHOALS OF MULLET, SEA BASS AND CUTTLEFISH.

OUR NEW RUSTIC FAMILY KITCHEN OVERLOOKS A QUIET CANAL WITHIN STROLLING DISTANCE OF THE GOTHIC HALLS OF THE RIALTO FISH MARKET. IT'S TIME TO FACE MY FEAR OF *FOLPETTI, MOECHE* AND *SCHILE*.

SERVIZIO
DI
COLLEGAMENTO

AEROPORTO → VENEZIA
(MARCO POLO)   (SAN MARCO)

AL VAPORETTO

ANNO 1984   — L. 9.500 —   SERIE Nº 01246

VENEZIA

SERIE   A

REPUBBLICA ITALIANA
MINISTERO PER I BENI CULTURALI E AMBIENTALI
UFFICIO CENTRALE PER I BENI AMBIENTALI,
ARCHITETTONICI, ARCHEOLOGICI, ARTISTICI E STORICI
BIGLIETTO D'INGRESSO

IL VISITATORE È TENUTO A CONSER...
ACQUISTATO, PRESSO LA BIGLIETTE...

S.ERASMO
KILO L.80

ENTRATA

PIOGGIA DI PESCI

In the early morning darkness a violent storm has crept over the Venetian lagoon. Once positioned over the warmth of the sleeping city this tempest unleashes its cold deluge. A ferocious downpour overwhelms the stone streets, rolling waves of thunder crack against the terracotta roofs. Rising above this battering rumble, rain thrashes down into the canal outside our kitchen window, like thousands of cold heavy arrows shot into the warm waters by an unseen army. Steam rises from the canal as it's violently shaken to life.

I wake, half expecting to dangle my arm off the bed and let it plop into cold water that covers the *terrazzo* floor, as if overnight a rising tide has snuck into our house unobserved, flooding the speckled marble floor with a cool, silent pool. Maybe one day Adriatic marine-life will get its own back on the city by re-inhabiting the flooded *calli*. Silver shoals of bream will dart through derelict windows as spider crabs scurry across sunken aquatic piazzas. Black clusters of mussels encrusting the dark, submerged kitchen furniture like gnarled, gothic wood carvings.

Rustled from my dream at seven o'clock by the melancholic church bells of Carmini tolling a few hundred yards from my warm pillow I remember I'm in our kitchen-living-room, sleeping on a pull-out bed. Today I'll be visiting the Rialto market for the first time as a cook with a family kitchen at hand.

My fear of fish, ichthyophobia, seems to stem rather irrationally from paper sharks and fish-bone traps concealed in innocent restaurant menus. Yet the effect of this phobia has manifested itself for decades in our kitchen, making it a fish-free zone. My earliest seafood memory is of eating *spaghetti con vongole* aged 7 cooked by my mother, Jos, on the garden terrace of our small rooftop apartment in Rome, overlooking the majestic stone expanse of the Piazza del Popolo. Hidden amongst the fresh *vongole* (clams) we'd bought in the Campo de' Fiori market were two miniature bright-red crabs who cleverly escaped from the kitchen table and skittered across the marble floor to become lost in the dark rooms. My mother later told me she'd found the stowaway crustacea and flushed them down the toilet, perhaps this added another facet to my ichthyophobia. Optimistically I chose to remember the positive part of the episode – enjoying clams. Venice is the perfect destination if you have a taste for shellfish. The lagoon is full of them, as are the fish markets and local trattorie.

On the final descent into Marco Polo airport I saw the *vongole* (clam) and *peocio* (mussel) farms criss-crossing the northern lagoon. In preparation I've started studying local fishing techniques and can make out lines of what must be fyke fish traps and trawlers. Hydraulic clam dredgers resemble praying mantises poised for the kill, their metal fishing gear up in the air like giant claws.

With this unexpected interest in fish and a need to explore seafood comes the cruel discovery that I feel completely lost around the whole subject. The cookbooks on our kitchen shelves brim with delicious seafood recipes and advice on gutting and filleting. Until now they had remained safely shut. And to reach my age without having owned a single copy of an Alan Davidson cookbook seems almost criminal, as foolish as visiting Venice without a map. Fortunately Venice is a city that positively embraces and encourages the notion of being lost, it's one of her major attractions. Being lost is a condition here that is both commonplace and happens daily. Perhaps it can become a strategy for exploring seafood and for enjoying the city at the same time.

My parents are living in Dorsoduro, a quiet residential neighbourhood full of students and Venetians. Dorsoduro is shaped like a shoe whose tip is the church of Santa Maria della Salute and the customs point beyond, and whose long stone sole is the Fondamenta Zattere, a wonderful place to walk and view sunsets. Dorsoduro is a *sestiere*, or borough, that somehow manages to maintain an everyday atmosphere of quietly getting on with its own business as it has done for centuries, a feat in itself in tourist-strewn Venice. Dorsoduro translates as 'hard back', which is reassuring out here on the water. The lagoon and surrounding marsh-lands have little or no sense of possessing a definable edge. Their boundaries change hourly, pushed by tides and diffused with light, presenting a challenge to someone like me who loves the dusty edge of a London kerb, or even better, a New York kerb-side rimmed with steel. *Acqua alta*, Venice's seasonal flooding, which bubbles up into the stone streets and lake-like piazzas, looms as a precursor for what global warming might bring to our coastal cities. Venetians are completely unfazed by these floods, leaving only tourists to worry.

To cope with this shifting liquid state Venetians possess mariners' eyes, bestowing them with an acute knowledge of their watery surroundings and the ability to pinpoint small islands the size of halibut, which miraculously appear far out in the lagoon during certain tides. The Venetian boatmen stand there, outside their boats, walking on water as you pass by gawping in amazement from a packed *vaporetto* bound for the Lido. During a heavy storm this sense of an indistinguishable edge embalms you as the fragile boundaries between land, sea and air disperse and merge, thrown together by the cascade of water. It's like being strapped to the mast of a rolling ship amidst a heavy squall. In Venetian style I always carry a small umbrella, although being drenched so quickly can be exhilarating.

My parents, Joe and Jos, were married in Venice in 1956 when both were young artists. Now their 48-year-old son, my wife, Jeff, and our 11-year-old daughter, Hannah, come to visit.

Such a family-filled future can't have been further from their thoughts all those years ago as they gazed romantically across to Dorsoduro from the island of Giudecca. Yet here we are, three generations sitting around a long wooden kitchen table planning what fish to buy for lunch.

As with previous family houses the focus of our new-found home is definitely the kitchen, and a companion cookbook quickly suggests itself, my parents and I have bought copies of Alan Davidson's *Mediterranean Seafood*, the perfect start to our Venetian library. For most cooks the view from their kitchen window is influential and hopefully restful, offering somewhere to glance whilst taking a break from chopping onions. We've never had a kitchen that faces the sea or a lake, so we feel completely spoilt by our new canal-side view. It's not a grand Venetian vista punctuated by *campanili* with the crispness of a Canaletto, nor does it overlook those distant haunting foggy expanses out across the flat silver lagoon. Its beauty is more rustic and in tune with our side of Dorsoduro. It reflects the way we like to cook – a gadget-free kitchen with a basic gas cooker flanked by two marble worktops each with a window that opens onto the canal four feet below. As I cook I can gaze into the jade-green water and watch a school of fish darting to safety under our neighbour's motor-boat. Looking to the left a small stone bridge arches across the canal. If someone is walking to the shops I can shout out a forgotten order for bread. We like to shop locally and on some visits never leave the neighbourhood at all except to walk to and from the airport bus-stop at Piazzale Roma. Without cars we learn to shop for food daily, which is a real joy.

It's hard to avoid seafood in Venice as I'm confronted by it daily. Our local restaurant, the wonderful Furatola, has a steamed-up front window display that is actually their cold-fish store – a proud display of local seafood, reminiscent of a sushi bar. When ordering supper the waiter proudly presents you with your chosen fish on a platter ready for inspection before it's whisked off and cooked to perfection. The window display allows me a glimpse of what they have bought fresh from the market. We tend to eat early, allowing time to chat to the owners. Unlike many other restaurants they have kept the tradition of having a small ante-chamber area as you enter, a space in which locals can come in and shelter from the weather and drink a glass of wine before returning home. Many trattorie have added a few extra tables at the expense of atmosphere and tradition.

I often fantasise about cooking the produce I encounter in foreign markets. We always take bag-loads back to London if a market is close enough to the airport. Now we're lucky enough to have a home kitchen within frying distance of the Pescheria fish market at the Rialto.

BIGOLI ALLE VONGOLE
BIGOLI WITH CLAMS

COOKING THIS DISH IN LONDON FOR OUR DAUGHTER, HANNAH, MAKES HER YEARN TO BE IN VENICE – EVOKING THE BELLS OF CARMINI AS THE PLATEFUL IS PLACED IN FRONT OF HER. SHE ASKS FOR BREAD TO DIP INTO THE DELICIOUS FISHY SAUCE.

Clams are so easy to cook. This dish is eaten up and down the coasts of Italy, but I particularly love the way it's served in Venice. They use a minute amount of tomato sauce – Venetians don't generally use tomatoes. Scattered across the pasta and clams are little green crystals or stars, which are, in fact flake like flecks of parsley. I must find out how they cut it quite so finely. I prefer to use a good quality dried spaghetti or *bigoli* in Venice rather than fresh pasta. I like it to have a little bite alongside the soft clams. *Linguine* is also good with clams. A small touch of fresh chilli can be delicious too.

SERVES 4

600g live, small hard-shelled clams
3 cloves garlic, finely chopped
1 onion, finely chopped
3 cherry tomatoes, finely chopped
320g bigoli *or spaghetti*

¼ glass dry white wine
2 tablespoons extremely finely chopped parsley

Scrub the clams then soak them for 1 hour in cold water to get rid of any grit or sand.

Before you prepare the tomato sauce put on a large pan of water to boil for your *bigoli*.

In a small pan, saute the garlic and onion in olive oil until translucent. Add the tomatoes, stir and simmer for 5 minutes.

Put the *bigoli* into the boiling water to cook. When it's almost done, cook the clams. Preheat a wide frying pan that has a lid. Rinse the clams in running water, then drop them into the hot pan, put on the lid and shake the clams around, cook for 15 seconds, then add the wine. The clams are cooked when their shells open, which only takes a minute or so. Remove half the clams with a slotted spoon. Scoop out the meat from these clams, discarding their shells, then return the clams to the pan.

Pour the tomato sauce over the clams and heat through briefly.

Strain the *bigoli* and stir it in with the clams and sauce.

Serve with unsalted bread. Do not add parmesan, just a scattering of parsley.

CARPET-SHELL CLAM
VENETIAN: *Caparassoli, caparozzoli*
ITALIAN: *Vongole verace*
SPECIES: *Tapes decussata (Linnaeus, 1758)*
FAMILY: *Veneridae (Venus Clams)*

MANILA CLAM, JAPANESE CARPET-SHELL, JAPANESE LITTLENECK
VENETIAN: *Caparassolo filippina*
ITALIAN: *Vongola filippin*
SPECIES: *Venerupis philippinarum (Adams & Reeve, 1850)*
FAMILY: *Veneridae (Venus Clams)*

Generally there are two types of clam – soft-shelled and hard-shelled. Clams are bi-valved, have double-hinged shells and like to live in sandy and muddy intertidal zones where they can burrow.

In the Mediterranean the indigenous carpet-shell clam has sadly been usurped by the farming of less tasty Manila clams. Introduced in 1983 to grow in the polluted waters, they flourished and aren't affected by algae blooms. The demand for clams has meant that aquaculture (farming) has overtaken fishing for wild clams. Farmed clams, unlike farmed fish, don't require wild fish (as fishmeal) or chemicals for their production. The main concern for cooks is to avoid clams which are dredged causing damage to the ocean floor, especially suction dredging – preferring clams that are hand-raked.

SEPPIE COL NERO CON POLENTA
CUTTLEFISH IN INK WITH POLENTA

This dish epitomises the simple beauty of Venetian cooking. I particularly like it when served with white polenta as it heightens the visual contrast, making it a black and white dish.

SERVES 3

1kg cuttlefish

2 cloves garlic, chopped

1 white onion, finely chopped

3 tablespoons olive oil

3 tablespoons finely chopped flat-leaf parsley

1 small glass white wine

1 sachet, 4g, of nero di seppia (squid/cuttlefish ink), optional

salt and pepper

white polenta

Prepare the cuttlefish by removing the beak, cuttlebone and carefully removing the guts, keep the small ink sacs whole and keep aside. Cut the flesh into thin strips and chop up the tentacles.

In a heavy pan gently saute the garlic and onion in oil until translucent. Then add the cuttlefish, parsley, white wine, ink sacs (or a sachet of *nero di seppia*) and season with salt and pepper.

Cover with a lid and simmer gently for about 40 minutes, stirring now and again. The aim is for a thick creamy sauce, this might require taking the lid off towards the end of cooking.

Serve with polenta. It makes fabulous leftovers.

White polenta is sold as pre-cooked slabs which can then be cut into 1 centimetre thick slices, brushed with olive oil and grilled for a few minutes each side. If you are lucky enough to have some white polenta flour you can make your own, in which case you can eat it runny.

CUTTLEFISH
VENETIAN: *Sepa*
ITALIAN: *Seppia*
SPECIES: *Sepia officinalis* (Linnaeus, 1758)
FAMILY: *Sepiidae* (Cuttlefish)

Cuttlefish have quite a short lifespan, about 18 months. The two main harvests of cuttlefish in the lagoon are April–May when they come from the open sea to lay eggs in the safety of the lagoon, and July–September when the young move out of the lagoon into the sea. The ink – sepia – has been used by artists for centuries.

SCHILE AGLIO E OGLIO
BROWN SHRIMP, OIL & GARLIC

The only fiddly part of this dish is the peeling of the shrimp. Some recipe books suggest that children are best at this, luck has it that I have two eleven-year-olds in the kitchen today. Hannah and her friend Abigail. Thanks girls. My parents cooked these last month and a few of the small shrimp jumped right out of the brown paper bag. *Schile* are often served in Venetian wine bars as delicate little snacks. I eat brown shrimp in London too, from Morecambe Bay in Lancashire where it's potted – little buttery tubs of wonder.

HANNAH KINDLY WENT OUT TO CAMPO SANTA MARGARITA TO SEE WHAT THE FISH STALLS HAD ON OFFER. THESE THREE STALLS CAN ONLY BE OWNED BY EX-FISHERMEN AND HAVE EXCELLENT LOCAL FISH. SHE CAME BACK WITH A BAGFUL OF HOPPING BROWN SHRIMP, IT LOOKED AS IF IT MIGHT WALK OFF THE TABLE AND OUT OF THE DOOR!

SERVES 4

BROWN SHRIMP
VENETIAN: *Schia, schila, schile*
ITALIAN: *Gambero della sabbia, gambero grigio*
SPECIES: *Crangon crangon (Linnaeus, 1758)*
FAMILY: *Crangonidae (Shrimps)*

Schile are the beautiful tiny brown shrimp found out in the lagoon. Like eating pumpkins or russet apples in the autumn, eating brown shrimp seems to reflect the autumnal surroundings of the dusky reed beds.

450g live brown shrimp
salt and pepper
olive oil
2 cloves garlic, finely chopped
2 tablespoons of extremely finely chopped parsley

Clean the shrimp carefully under running water, don't let any jump behind the cooker!

Put on a large pan of water to boil. Once it's reached a rolling boil put in all the shrimp. Bring back to a boil, it will froth up. Cook for 3 minutes.

Drain and carefully peel the shrimp.

Season with a touch of salt and a few turns of black pepper. Dress with olive oil, garlic and parsley.

Served cold with grilled polenta slices or on thin slices of toast.

garusoli

We threw him in a the shrimp canal

shrimp

Fred

R.I.P fred the shrimp the poor

FOLPETTI LESSI CONDITI MINI OCTOPUS

THESE ARE THE WONDERFUL MINI OCTOPUS SNACKS, *CICHETI,* SERVED IN VENETIAN WINE BARS. PERFECT FOR A PRE-SUPPER SNACK OR A LUNCHTIME NIBBLE.

There are so many fantastic seafood dishes that sidestep the problems of filleting, fish bones or judging exactly when a grilled sole is ready. I'm beginning to think I could happily focus my seafood kitchen on molluscs alone. It's a scientific genus that includes all manner of delicate clams, mussels, oysters, the versatile cuttlefish, squid and octopus. All tasty, easy to prepare and eaten along coastlines around the world, so I'm even learning transferable culinary skills – brilliant.

CURLED OCTOPUS
VENETIAN: *Folpo*
ITALIAN: *Moscardino bianco*
SPECIES: *Eledone cirrosa*
(Lamarck, 1798)
FAMILY: *Octopodidae*
(Octopus)

Curled octopus are found in the Atlantic Ocean, the English Channel, the North Sea and the Mediterranean Sea.

SERVES 4

12 small curled octopuses
2 bay leaves
1 rib celery, chopped
1 carrot, peeled and chopped
salt and pepper

3 lemons, 1 cut in half, remainder cut into wedges
3 tablespoons olive oil
1 handful flat-leaf parsley, very finely chopped

Remove the eyes, beak, and internal organs of each octopus, wash the rest thoroughly.

Bring a large pan of water to a rolling boil. Add the bay leaves, celery, carrot, seasoning and half a lemon to the water.

Each octopus needs to be dipped briefly into the water, to curl its tentacles before further cooking. This is done by holding each octopus with pincers, then plunging it into the boiling water for a few seconds. Watch as the tentacles curl, then pull the octopus out of the water briefly so it will hold its curled shape, then drop it back into the water to finish cooking. Continue dipping and curling until all of the octopuses are cooking in the pot. Boil for 20–30 minutes.

Leave the octopus to cool in the water, then drain, discarding the stock vegetables.

Cut the octopuses into small pieces and serve with olive oil, lemon wedges, pepper and parsley. These are also good on squares of white polenta.

MERCATO DEL PESCE AL MINUTO.

PESCHERIA

MOSCARDINI VIVI NOSTRANI

Like other camera-wielding visitors to Venice, the must-see gastronomic spots I'm consistently drawn to are the two markets at the Rialto: the Pescheria and the Erberia in our neighbouring *sestiere* San Polo. Until now I've only been able to casually appreciate their wares through my camera lens or by eating *fritto misto* or *polenta con seppie* in local trattorie. Today that will change. I'm only a pocketful of euros and a *vaporetto* number 1 away from my first slippery bagful of Venetian seafood to take home and cook for my family. Being a seafood novice I might avoid the bony end of the spectrum and search out a mixture of manageable sized fish, adding some molluscs for safety and easy cooking.

It's an early Thursday morning in late July and Jeff has already been out walking and exploring in the damp streets, enjoying the traffic-free soundscape. She comes back to pick me up, leaving Hannah asleep in the house with her grandparents. We step out into a fresh summer morning. The yellow ochre walls of our house are still cold and damp with dew. A view of Carmini can be seen through the branches of a tree growing in our neighbour's walled garden. A cool breeze creeps and winds through the tangle of streets. You can rarely see the end of a Venetian *calle*, unless it's short. These snarled, knotted alleys are laid out with such a wonderful irregularity that an elbow, twist or junction will often block the view ahead, obscuring the destination. Even after you've built a mental map of a street it has other ways to confuse and disorientate you. As the shops close for lunch they act like hermit crabs retreating inside their shells – all traces of what was on sale vanish and the facades merge with the surrounding architecture, a perfect camouflage.

Unlike most cities, Venice lacks the reassuring hierarchy of widening street-sizes to lead you to major thoroughfares. A narrow crack of an alley is just as likely to end at the nearest *vaporetto* stop. The arrivals of *vaporetti* at Cà Rezzonico ahead of us can be felt as trickles of workers walk past us from each arriving waterbus. A *vaporetto* number 1 is idling its engine as we reach the embarkation platform, propellers churning the pale green water. This early morning boat is almost empty for the short trip to the Rialto. A few early-bird tourists are pecking at warm marmalade-filled croissants in hotel restaurants along the Riva del Ferro overlooking the Grand Canal. The bridge-and-ferry crowds haven't yet descended from the mainland car parks at Tronchetto, the Fusina camping grounds or from the moored super cruiser vessels at Stazione Marittima, each the size of a New York housing project.

The pale rising sun touches us briefly as we descend the Rialto steps into the purple cool of the market streets, past the church of San Giacomo di Rialto, supposedly consecrated on 25 March 421, the same day Venice was founded. Cutting diagonally across this *campo* in the distance we see the Erberia, the fruit and vegetable market – an exotic forest of colours under a powder blue sky. The seasonal wares of the Erberia are saturated with vivid reds, bitter purples, startling yellows and every shade of green imaginable – from brilliant limes to an olive-green so dark it's almost black. Stall-holders wash lettuce and apricots in the fountain, picking out bad leaves and discarding rotten fruit. Finished stacks of *zucchini* and *melanzane* are refreshed with a final spray of water. But today our destination is the Pescheria di Rialto, housed in two canal-side mock-gothic halls, built in 1907 to replace a 19th-century metal and glass building which was demolished after only ten years because Venetians didn't like it. The new long hall sits alongside a narrow canal where fish crates are unloaded from boats by crane and then wheeled through open arches. We step into the dark smaller second hall whose arches overlook the Grand Canal. Red and green tarpaulin banners trap the delicate shade and block out the growing heat. Low strung portable work-lights are looped and clipped above rows of trestle tables piled high with ice on which fish merchants are skilfully arranging their day's purchases from the commercial markets at either Chioggia in the southern lagoon, or Mercato Ittico Il Tronchetto, by Piazzale Roma. Thankfully the trappings of these commercial markets filter through to the Rialto, preserving a sense of market-day impermanence. Although the fish used to be sold from metal trays on the pavement there are still no built-in chilled displays and even the surrounding shops erect temporary tables each morning for their fresh fish. Once the stalls have been dismantled only an occasional discarded fish head from a *coda di rospo* (monkfish) alerts you to the bustling market that had been in action a few hours before.

Our eyes slowly adjust to the dimness, perfect for viewing what should be seen fathoms below the surface of the sea, the fish are luminescent. Most of the fish on sale at Rialto are left whole and un-gutted, let alone filleted, this is how locals like them. Eels, crabs and crustacea are most definitely alive. At first I wander around with my camera like a shark circling its prey. Jeff goes off to buy vegetables. Photography over the past few years has been a useful introduction to the fish on display here, but my mind now clicks into a different way of looking as I grapple with the questions of what to buy and cook. How much does it cost? How will it taste and smell?

There's also a tangible association to nature, a sense of wild foraged food and of hunter gatherers. Fish are a natural resource that few of us ever see in the wild, unlike the occasional wild mushroom, roadside fennel plant or bramble bush. I don't feel this connection to the sea in a London supermarket or fishmonger no matter how fresh the fish are. Here I feel a visceral link to the very bottom of the Adriatic sea, enhanced perhaps by the lapping waters of the Grand Canal and the sound of squawking seagulls and boats chugging by. Fish have been sold on this site for over six centuries.

Stepping into the Pescheria requires you to adopt several languages. A multi-lingual lexicon of fish. Venetians have a baffling array of words to describe their seafood. Boxes of seemingly identical small crabs all come with different names. Jeff has returned with a bag of Sant Erasmo salad and notices intriguing text on the fish price labels, the letters FAO, followed by a number. *Pescato – Zona FAO no 37.2 Mediterraneo* or *Zona FAO no 34 Atlantico Centro Orientale*. We assume this is where the fish were caught so search out Mediterranean or Adriatic fish amongst the signs. Jeff makes a note of which zone applies to each fish we buy, I can research the significance of FAO later. Most of the squid are caught in the Atlantic but we manage to find Adriatic *calamari* (squid) on a stall specialising in locally caught fish, labelled *nostrani*, which in Venetian means 'ours' or 'local'. I want to try the pre-cooked *gamberi* (common prawn), you can buy them live if you feel a lobster moment coming on – like the live hopping *schiele* (brown shrimp) my father, Joe, bought last week in Campo Santa Margarita. Next I find some twisted candy-shaped molluscs called *garusoli* (also used to make a purple dye), which I've never heard of. The fishmonger suggests immersing them in cold water, bringing to the boil and simmering for 25 minutes. I buy a puppy-sized *scampo* (Dublin bay prawn) for Hannah to draw later and, finally, some fish to fry and bake. A handful of slippery *sardine* (sardines), quite large which would make them pilchards in England, some medium sized *acciughe* (anchovies), and a bagful of what looks like whitebait, *latterini*, which will cook in an instant and won't require gutting or boning. Two bagfuls of gastronomic promise and a thousand questions swimming in my head. I need a map to aid me, or at least a cappuccino and a cake before returning home to cook. As with any new cooking venture some special implements might be required. We go home via Calle Nobleni to buy a big frying pan and some tongs. Our kitchen is at the 'if-you-need-an-implement-buy-it' stage.

LUNGHEZZE MINIME PERMESSE
PER LA VENDITA DEL PESCE
DELLE SEGUENTI QUALITÁ

	CENT.
BARBON. TRIA. SARDELLA. SARDON	7
BRANZIN. ORADA. DENTAL. CORBO	
SPARO. BOTOLO. BOSEGHETI. SOASO	
LOTREGAN. MECIATO. VERZELATA	12
LOVO. SFOGIO. PASSARIN. ROMBO	
BISATO.	25
OSTREGA	5
PEOCIO.	3

RISOTTO CON I GO
GOBY RISOTTO

16.00

AT THE MARKET THE *GO* WERE FRESH, STILL GASPING IN SOME COLD AUTUMN AIR. IT WAS RAINING SO HARD PERHAPS THE FISH THOUGHT THEY WERE STILL UNDERWATER. VENICE SEEMS TO RETREAT TO THE SEA IN SUCH WEATHER.

I'm not woken at six by the bells of Carmini but by the doleful moans of a fog-horn emanating from a cruise-ship as she leaves the safety of the quayside at Stazione Marittima and heads out into the deep waters of the Canale di Giudecca. Leaning out of the kitchen window the canal view is like a river at dawn, hung with dense fog and trails of rising mist. As the church bells toll seven o'clock a series of haunting, melancholic notes punctuate the passing of another vessel in the opposite direction. These vast cruise ships look otherworldly, as if they're carrying souls somewhere other than Athens. Their pristine white hulls dotted with cabin windows and balconies look like the stacked marble tombs on the cemetery island of San Michele. I'm tempted to dash up to our terrace to see if I can see one of these leviathans pass by the end of our canal, but I know the view will be obscured by the dense fog. It's also dark. As daylight tries to break I think of wintry fish, in particular goby or *go*. To experience *go* properly I want to cook some fish whole and use others to make a stock for risotto. These fish seem to embody the colours of the wintry lagoon locked in fog. A risotto made with goby stock is subtle, calming and tranquil, not like the delicious but rather too salty stock made with crustacea, crab and shrimp that we had in the Trattoria Alla Madonna last night. The aim of my recipe is to use an undervalued local fish, try a local little-used fish yourself.

GRASS GOBY, WEED GOBY

VENETIAN: *Go, maciarea (young)*
ITALIAN: *Ghiozzo*
SPECIES: *Zosterisessor ophiocephalus (Pallas, 1814)*
FAMILY: *Gobiidae (Gobies)*

There are 57 species of this fish family in the Mediterranean and Black Sea. The tasty variety we find in the Rialto fish market are adorned with a lagoon colouring – rather like a Venetian camouflage.

SERVES 4

For the fish stock
1 go, gutted and cleaned
1 onion
1 carrot
1 bay leaf
700ml water

For the go
1 onion, sliced
3 go, gutted and cleaned
1 tablespoon white wine vinegar
salt and pepper

For the risotto
250g Vialone nano *risotto rice*
2 onions, finely chopped
1 tablespoon olive oil
300ml go fish stock

The stock

In a pan add the *go*, carrot, onion, bay leaf and water. Simmer for 15 minutes, strain and set aside.

The risotto

Wash the rice in a sieve under cold running water, working it with your fingers. Let it drain. Meanwhile, fry the onion in olive oil in a wide, heavy frying pan until translucent. Add the rice and stir it with a flat wooden spoon until it is coated with oil.

In another pan, fry the onion slices until brown. Remove the onions and set aside, add the three *go*, vinegar, salt and pepper to the pan. Simmer, covered, for 20 minutes.

Meanwhile, finish the risotto. Add the *go* fish stock slowly, stirring gently, loosening the rice on the bottom of the pan. Finally add water a bit at a time to keep the risotto moist until the rice is cooked *al dente* with some bite to it. The risotto should still be slightly wet, and should almost pour onto a plate rather than fall in a heap.

Add the onion slices to the pan-fried *go* and serve on top the risotto. Serve with radicchio.

MUSSELS & CANNELLINI WITH PASTA

OUR VENETIAN FRIEND DANIELA COOKS A PUGLIESE DISH USING MUSSELS AND TWO PASTA SHAPES SMOTHERED IN CANNELLINI BEANS - A PERFECT DISH FOR WHEN IT'S STILL CHILLY ON THE TERRACE.

Daniela and Mariella arrive at 6.00, ahead of Enzo and Assunta at 7.30. Mario arrives at 8.30 because half way along the Grand Canal, Assunta remembered she hadn't fed their dog, so Mario kindly went back to feed him. To my shame I must admit to never having made pasta before at the age of 48. Attempting *orecchiette* is jumping in at the deep end and requires four or five hand movements – no machines – any one of which done wrong will ruin your pasta shape. At first glance it looks baffling and tricky but after several attempts, some ending on the floor, we get the hang of it, which is extremely rewarding. Mum, and dad help out too. We also make *ferretti* shapes using a *ferretta*. The finished dish is a sheer delight – a dense thick sauce dotted with mussels with shapes echoing each other. Amazingly by 10.30 I'm asleep on my kitchen bed.

SERVES 10

MUSSEL
VENETIAN: *Peocio, peocchia, pedocchi, peochio dell'Arsenale*
ITALIAN: *Mitilo, muscolo, cozza*
SPECIES: *Mytilus galloprovincialis (Lamarck, 1819)*
FAMILY: *Mytilidae (Sea Mussels)*

REGIONE del VENETO

300g orecchiette-*shaped pasta*
2 x 500g cans cannellini beans
6 cloves garlic, finely chopped
4 tablespoons olive oil

15 cherry tomatoes,
  cut in half
1.2 kg live mussels

Put on a big pan of water to cook the pasta.

In a small pan heat the cannellini beans, mash about three quarters of them and add a little water if too dry. Keep warm.

Add the pasta to the boiling water.

In a wide, deep frying pan saute the garlic in olive oil then add the tomatoes and cook for 5 minutes or so. Squash them a little but not too much, they need to retain some of their shape and not be too pulpy.

Pile the mussels on top of the tomatoes. Cover with a lid. Bring up to a boil, stir and shake the pan. The mussels are cooked once the shells have opened.

Take the pan off the heat. Remove at least half of the mussel shells, throwing out any mussels that haven't opened.

Put the pan back on a gentle heat until the pasta has finished cooking.

Drain the pasta then heap it into the mussel frying pan, stir.

Now use the mashed cannellini beans to thicken the sauce, stirring them all in. Serve in a wide soup bowl. Best eaten with a spoon.

CANNELLINI CON PASTA E COZZE

WHEN IS A FISH NOT A FISH

I gaze down at the canal through the kitchen window whilst unpacking our Rialto bags. A neighbour opposite throws out stale bread onto the still surface of the water. The bread lands with a pap and within four seconds a huge seagull swoops down and grabs it up before three other birds arrive to squabble over the next soggy morsel.

Never in my life have I faced such a variety of seafood to cook – I feel excited rather than scared, but still lost. Fish are so inseparable from Venetian cuisine that the city's first published cookbook omitted recipes for fish altogether, assuming that everyone knew how to cook anything caught at sea or fished from the lagoon. For a wary fish-cook such as myself Venetian food is reassuringly unpretentious and simple to prepare, born out of an honest approach to seasonal ingredients from their islands, its lagoon and the Adriatic beyond.

Some of the fish we've bought have Italian names, some Venetian. Local fish names might be used elsewhere in the Veneto, some aren't used beyond Piazzale Roma, whereas others might persist along the Emilia-Romagna coastline. I feel the need to identify what we've bought in English, if only to be able to consult a few cookbooks. Many old cookbooks won't even suggest a particular species of fish for a recipe, their indexes don't delve into the subject beyond a listing for 'fish'. Venice has such a singular approach to cooking that knowing what you're eating, or cooking, is important. Our cookbooks need to be as much an identification field guide as a recipe book, and that's where Alan Davidson's books win me over. Using taxonomy he organises his seafood books by ocean or sea and then by family and by scientific order. Absolutely brilliant. With hundreds of fish to choose from they benefit greatly from being organised by family, especially when the destination is the kitchen. Grouping fish by family means they share common physiological attributes, such as bone structure or suitability for grilling. Using such a book educates your palate as well as developing fish identifying skills. I would like to have an additional classification of fish by boney-ness. As my mother consults Alan Davidson's *Mediterranean Seafood*, I crosscheck using Jeffrey Steingarten's *The Man Who Ate Everything* which has a Venetian-Italian-English glossary of fish names at the Rialto. My father has a *Venetian dialect dictionary* at hand. As a restaurant goer in Venice I find *polpi*, *folpi*, *seppie* and *calamari* all seem to coalesce as a single species when on a plate of sizzling *fritto misto*. Yet trying to identify the ingredients to buy and cook for a *fritto misto* is troublesome and if attempting to write down a

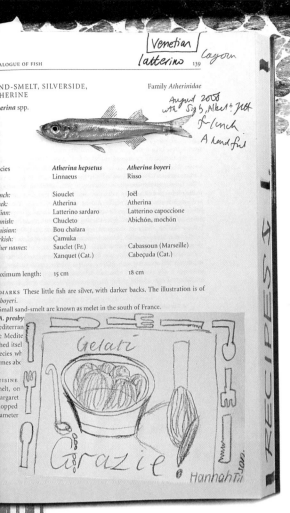

Venetian latterino cagörn 139

ND-SMELT, SILVERSIDE,
HERINE

erina spp.

Family *Atherinidae*

August 2008 with Sig b, Albert + Jeff for lunch. A handful

cies	*Atherina hepsetus* Linnaeus	*Atherina boyeri* Risso
nch:	Siouclet	Joël
ek:	Atherina	Atherina
ian:	Latterino sardaro	Latterino capoccione
nish:	Chucleto	Abichón, mochón
isian:	Bou chaïara	
kish:	Çamuka	
er names:	Sauclet (Fr.)	Cabassoun (Marseille)
	Xanquet (Cat.)	Cabeçuda (Cat.)
ximum length:	15 cm	18 cm

MARKS These little fish are silver, with darker backs. The illustration is of
boyeri.
mall sand-smelt are known as melet in the south of France.

A. presby
editerran
e Medite
hed itsel
ecies wh
mes abc

UISINE
melt, on
argaret
opped
ameter

recipe problems with fish names implode. The popular dish *spaghetti al nero di seppia* is usually translated outside of Italy as 'spaghetti with squid ink', a poor translation as *seppia* are cuttlefish, not squid. Sachets of cuttlefish ink are often mislabelled as squid ink, perhaps it sounds more appealing? This mis-labelling is then transferred to recipe names globally, perpetuating the error, or maybe it's just poor translation or marketing. The surprisingly useful book, *The Multilingual Dictionary of Fish and Fish Products*, lists *nero di seppia* as being the ink from Cephalopoda, which means it could be ink from either squid, octopus or cuttlefish. No wonder I'm confused as to whether *seppia* are squid or *calamari* are octopus rings. The world of naming fish in multiple markets across many nations is bewildering. A lone photograph I took several years ago at the Rialto of *zotoli* doesn't seem to appear in either the Davidson or Steingarten books, like a stray piece of forensic evidence. So I start to put together *Jake's Rialto Reckoner*, a visual field guide to what to buy at the Rialto market, to help me reconcile and record all the various names and images of fish I've gathered over the years. I consult a recent book purchase, *Pesci molluschi e crostacei della laguna di Venezia* but still no *zotoli*. My list remains full of holes.

I'm relieved to find that I enjoy standing in front of a frying pan of small fish spluttering in oil, with a glass of wine in hand and a family eagerly awaiting the next batch. Some of my happiest times have been spent in kitchens and this one is definitely high on my list. I gaze down into the murky green depths of the canal through the kitchen window just to check that it's still real. I'm amazed at how little work is needed to transform our Rialto fish into a table of delights, all delicious. Next time I'll make sure I have the triad of standard fish cooking supplements at hand: flat-leafed parsley, plenty of lemons and plain white flour. As I settle in for a siesta my mind is still pounding with questions, unfathomable for the time being.

Back in London as I walk down an ornately decorated staircase in the Victoria and Albert Museum while looking for the entrance to the Reyner Banham Memorial Lecture, I notice an ochre ceramic relief with the name Linnaeus on it. Carolus Linnaeus is considered the father of modern taxonomy. I don't often come across scientific names when cooking and I've never felt the urge to know why the scientific name for a chicken is *Gallus gallus*. When I find chicken in a recipe that's usually as much information as I need. Seafood unfortunately throws up so many different problems, especially when buying it abroad, or finding fish from distant oceans at my local fishmonger. At the Rialto they even list the region of sea it was caught in – as overseen by the FAO – I discover FAO is the Food and Agriculture Organization of the United Nations. Fish identification becomes an issue not only for the cook but also for the planet. For naming fish I need solid unambiguous ground. Taxonomy offers it, thanks to Linnaeus.

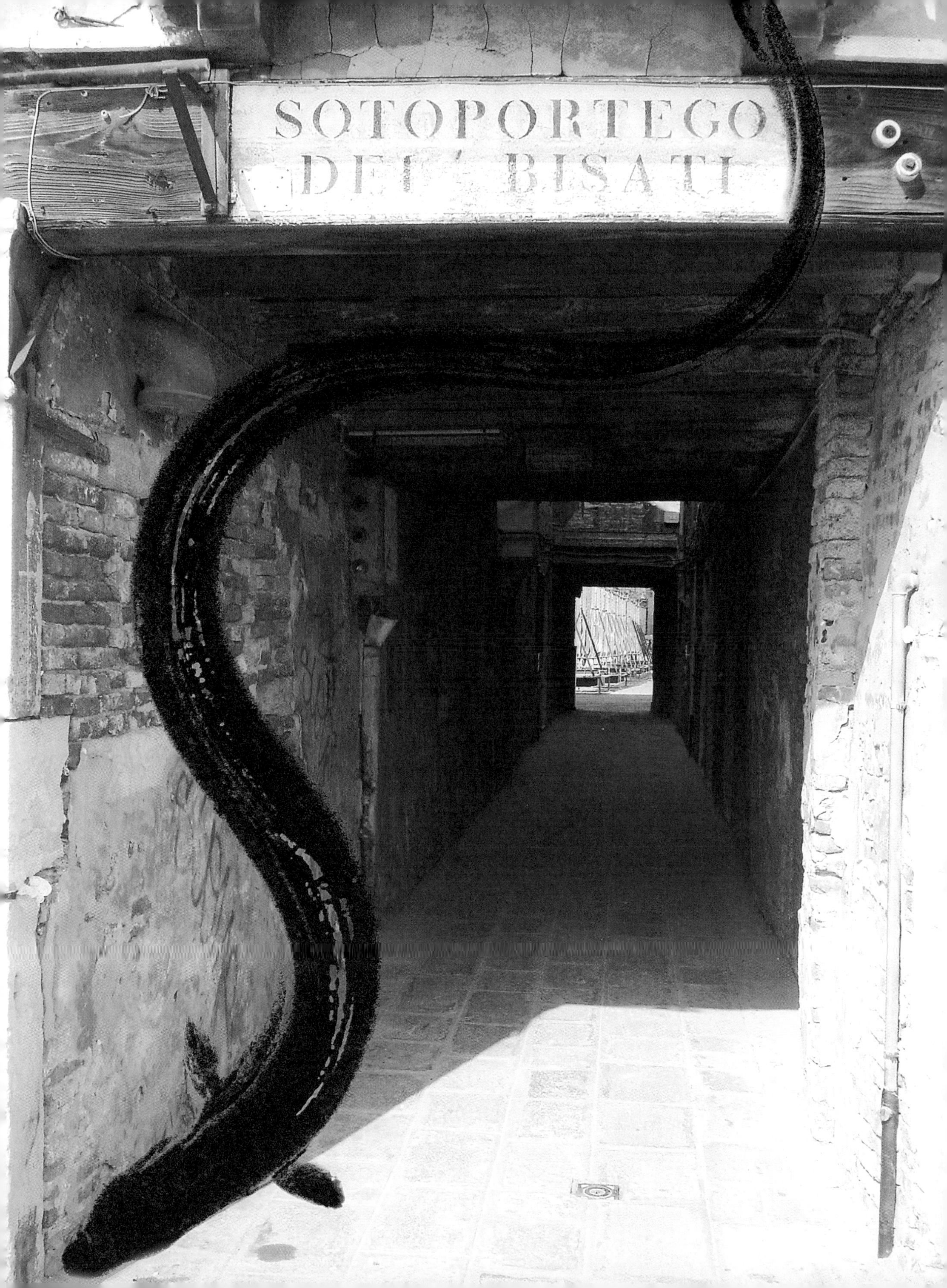
SOTOPORTEGO
DEI BISATI

ZOTOLI CON SPAGHETTI
DWARF BOBTAIL WITH SPAGHETTI

WHEN COMPILING A LIST OF PHOTOGRAPHS OF EVERY SPECIES ON SALE AT THE PESCHERIA I COME ACROSS A STRANGE PHOTO I TOOK A FEW YEARS AGO OF A MINIATURE CUTTLEFISH – I WONDER IF IT'S A JUVENILE OR JUST SMALL? TODAY THE MYSTERY CEPHALOPOD IS BACK IN THE MARKET. WHAT ARE THEY AND HOW DO I COOK THEM? MY MOTHER COMES TO THE RESCUE AFTER ASKING IN THE NEIGHBOURHOOD.

Some locals we ask in Dorsoduro don't know what *zotoli* are.
In the afternoon Hannah and Mum were off buying *prosecco spento* and asked the lady in the wine shop how to cook *zotoli*. A well-dressed Venetian lady in a fine pink overcoat who is an expert on *cucina Veneziana* overheard and said 'Ah you mean *zotoeti*, we also call ladies who dress in an old-fashioned way *zoto*.' She kindly goes on to explain there are two ways to cook *zotoeti*. Use them in risotto or fry them whole in olive oil with a touch of garlic and an obligatory scattering of parsley, added at the last minute, not before, as it makes the herb taste bitter. Serve with *fettucine* or *tagliolini*. Sounds fabulous. Around the Mediterranean these little *seppie* are often deep-fried, in France they're called *suppions frits*.

Hunting for more mini-cuttlefish species in other culinary zones might help me unearth more recipes but requires a little malacology, the scientific study of molluscs. Looking at the *zotoli's* family tree opens up a wide, wild world. The broader family, Decapodiformes, contains about 95 genera with 450 species in 31 families. Slightly closer in, the Sepiolidae family has three subfamilies and 13 genera and contains about 55 species, which are between 1–10cm long. The other 13 members of the *zotoli* family are particularly common in the Mediterranean and eastern Atlantic Ocean from western Africa up to Norway, but can also be found on the western edge of the Pacific. The *Sepiola atlantica*, Dwarf bobtail, Mickey mouse squid, Dumpling squid or Stubby squid, is found around Britain. In Asia similar cuttlefish can be found along the western margin of the Pacific Ocean from Singapore up to the South Kuril Islands north of Japan, they stay within the continental shelf. I'm afraid my newfound knowledge of Sepiolidae will only be used to find interesting ways to cook them.

Hannah notices how cute they look, rather like a Japanese cartoon character with big bulbous eyes, maybe *zotoli* should have their own range of notebooks, ringtones and mobile phone covers. Supper is *zotoli* with spaghetti, *sgombro* fillets in oil and *uove de seppie* (cuttlefish eggs). After supper we watch *Some Like It Hot*.

DWARF BOBTAIL
VENETIAN: *Zotoli, zotoeti, zotoleto, zotolo*
ITALIAN: *Babuccia, babbucciedda, beccaficu, calamaretto, cape'e chiuove, malnascui, porpo-seppia, scarpetta, scartoccio, seccetella, sepietta, sepiola, sepiolina, seppetta, sponce currienti, totanino, tutariedde*
SPECIES: *Sepiola rondeleti* (Steenstrup, 1856)
FAMILY: *Sepiolidae* (Cuttlefish)

These minute cuttlefish unlike larger cuttlefish can be found in most oceans and are more widely distributed as they can be found in deep-sea benthic and even mesopelagic habitats. Their small size means they are usually a bycatch where fisheries are targeting other species. I found an Atlantic bobtail hidden in a bag of brown shrimp from Morecombe Bay on the west coast of England. Venice is the only fish market I have seen them for sale other than at Tsukiji in Japan. The spawning season extends from March through November in the western Mediterranean.

SERVES 4

300g spaghetti
1 tablespoon olive oil
1 large handful zotoli, *cleaned, gutted and*
  most of the ink sacs removed
2 cloves garlic, chopped
2 tablespoons finely chopped flat-leaf parsley
pepper or **peperoncino**
extra virgin olive oil

Put on a large pan of water to cook the pasta. When the water is boiling put in the spaghetti.

In a wide frying pan gently fry the *zotoli* and garlic in olive oil for about 4 minutes, throw in the parsley, stir once and take the pan off the heat.

As soon as the spaghetti is cooked, drain it and heap into the frying pan, stirring to gather up all the juices of the *zotoli*.

Serve with a twist or two of pepper or *peperoncino* and a long drizzle of your best peppery virgin olive oil.

SARDE IN SAOR
SWEET & SOUR SARDINES

Marinating fried sardines and onions in vinegar and oil as a way to preserve fish is a technique that originated here in the 14th century. Traditionally they were served from gondolas on the eve of the Festa del Redentore, the third Saturday in July. Sole or flounder are also used and more recently I heard of sea bream being marinated at the restaurant Da Fiore. I found sea bream fillets too big alongside the onion and sultanas. The dish is eaten cold.

SERVES 4

4 whole sardines (450g), gutted, cleaned, heads and tails off
2 tablespoons plain white flour
sunflower or rapeseed oil
½ teaspoon salt

1 white onion, sliced into rings
2 tablespoons white wine vinegar
2 tablespoons white wine
1 teaspoon pine nuts
2 teaspoons sultanas
grated zest of ½ orange

You can choose whether or not to fillet the fish, they're often left whole with just their heads and tails removed.

Dust the fish lightly with flour and fry them gently in a little sunflower oil, 5 minutes each side, or until cooked. Don't use olive oil, it would be too strong a flavour. The fish must not get crispy. Drain well and season with salt. Throw out the cooking oil and clean the pan.

Fry the onions in a little more sunflower oil until translucent, not golden. Pour in the vinegar, wine, pine nuts, sultanas and grated orange zest. Simmer for a few minutes.

Find a glass or ceramic dish with a lid that will accommodate the fish. Place two fish in the dish, cover with some onions and sauce, add the other fish and cover with the remaining onions and sauce.

Cool and refrigerate. Allow to rest for at least 24 hours, preferably for a few days.

Good served with grilled polenta and salad.

EUROPEAN PILCHARD
VENETIAN: *Palassiola, renga, renghetta, sardon*
ITALIAN: *Sardina*
SPECIES: *Sardina pilchardus* (Walbaum, 1792)
FAMILY: *Clupeidae* (Herrings, Shads, Sardines, Menhadens)

In the UK a sardine is a young pilchard. Elsewhere it's likely to be another species altogether, such as the Pacific sardine (*Sardinops sagax*). On the European continent the name almost implies a size of small fish rather than a species.

SACCO DA PESCHERIA
PESCHERIA BAGFUL

Six small bags of assorted seafood from the Pescheria means I can try different cooking methods, frying, baking and boiling. The entire meal will be served on an eat-it-when-it's-cooked basis, the main purpose is exploration. All this work is helped along with slugs of *prosecco spento* from our local wine shop, one of the dwindling shops that sell loose wine. Heavy, deep shelves are stacked with large demijohns attached to petrol station nozzles, wine is decanted into recycled 1.5 litre *aqua minerale* bottles. Local restaurants give it the fancier name of *prosecco tranquillo*. Perfect for a lunchtime drink that won't require a long siesta to sleep off.

SERVES 5

mazzancole *(prawns)*	*salad*
calamari *(squid)*	*bread*
garusoli *(murex)*	**peperoncino**
sarde *(sardines)*	*olive oil*
alici *(anchovies)*	*lemons*
latterini *(sand-smelt)*	*plain white flour, or fine couscous*

A bowlful of salad sits on the table with a long loaf of bread. This will keep everyone happy and fill in any gaps whilst I cook. The fish is served in batches straight out of the pan.

The striped *mazzancole* (prawns) are seriously succulent, sweet and extremely easy to cook as they helpfully change colour from grey to pink when cooked after a few minutes in the pan. I add a touch of *peperoncino* to the last few for Dad, he adores chilli.

Next comes the squid. I remove the eyes, intestines, one bone - which is like a transparent quill – and the skin, which peels away easily. I'm left with two wings, tentacles and a large pouch-like sack. Squid requires brief cooking otherwise it feels and tastes like rubber. I slice them into strips and fry for 45 seconds in a touch of olive oil, a quick divine appetiser.

The *garusoli* (murex) when boiled for 20 minutes remind me rather of whelks or snails.

Sarde e alici (sardines and anchovies), being so small, makes them perfect training for gutting and de-boning, all done with small, sharp knives. I bake the larger sardines, splayed like butterflies, on a bed of chopped tomatoes and sliced garlic for about 15–20 minutes.

The smallest fish are so tiny they can be eaten whole, bones and all. We're out of flour, so I dust the *latterini* (sand-smelt) and *alici* (anchovies) with some extra-fine couscous. It made lousy couscous last night but makes an interesting flour substitute today. I fry until crisp, a few minutes each side, and serve instantly. To eat fish bones is thrilling and empowering to someone who has been paranoid about them for decades, definitely part of a 'graduated exposure therapy'.

SEPPIOLINE, SALSICCE E SALVIA IN BRODO

SAUSAGE STUFFED CUTTLEFISH SOUP

CUTTLEFISH
SEE: *page 18*

We ask Daniela for a good butcher, she recommends Laguna Carne on the corner of the fish market, near the spice shop Mascari. We scan the stalls and shops on a bright winter's morning after alighting at the newly installed *vaporetto* 1 stop, Rialto Mercato, a great idea.

IT'S TIME TO TRY SOME FIDDLY FISH, AND TO USE A GREAT DOUBLE ACT, PORK AND SEAFOOD, AS FOUND IN A THAI FISH SOUP SUCH AS *KAENG CHERD PLA MUK YUD SY.* USING THE STRUCTURE OF THE THAI DISH I LOOK FOR SUITABLE VENETIAN INGREDIENTS : STUFFED SMALL CUTTLEFISH, STEAMED, SERVED IN A FISH BROTH WITH MUSHROOMS.

The stop operates from 8am–2pm. At the end of our shopping trip we spy a white tray of *seppie* with some extremely small specimens hiding in the corner. The stallholder digs around and finds ten cuttlefish for us. Perfect. The fish stall also has three *coda de rospo* (monkfish) heads. At first he was unwilling to sell them to us, he prefers to sell them to restaurants. Dad charms him. We also buy *zotoli* and *seppie uovo*. Cleaning the *seppiolini* is a tricky business, pulling off the head and tentacles, trying to get out the ink sacs, cuttlebones and innards. It's especially difficult as I need to be stuffing what isn't much bigger than a large olive. As a test I remove the skin from some, not others. The skinned cuttlefish are harder to stuff and require a small wooden toothpick to hold them together. The unskinned cuttlefish once cooked are fine, and are easier to stuff. The butcher Laguna Carne has beautiful pork sausages. He tells us they are filled with hand-chopped pork, no machines. It's like eating a pork chop.

SERVES 5

1 Italian pork sausage, or some pork, cooked
1 clove garlic, crushed
3 sage leaves, finely chopped
10 small cuttlefish, cleaned, gutted, ink sacs and cuttlebone removed
¾ litre fish or light, clear chicken stock
6 mushrooms, sliced

Chop the precooked sausage finely and mix in the garlic and sage. Carefully stuff this mixture into the cuttlefish with a small teaspoon. Place in a steamer basket, covered, and steam over boiling water for 15 minutes.

In a pan, heat up the chicken or fish stock, add water to taste and simmer gently for 5 minutes, adding the sliced mushrooms for the last minute or two.

I like to use a Chinese soup bowl, narrow and tall, not wide and flat. Place two cuttlefish in each soup bowl, ladle over the soup and mushrooms.

CRAB HUNT

Our slow assimilation into this new culinary playground is definitely becoming a team adventure for all the family. When I'm not in Venice I catch up with seasonal goodies on offer at the markets by speaking to my mother on the phone. She keeps me in touch with new dishes they've discovered in restaurants in Dorsoduro or at friends' houses, taking photos which she posts to me. So by the time Hannah and I arrive one cold crisp day in April I feel fully briefed with what's on offer, hopefully small soft-shell crabs, called *moeche* in Venetian. I've never bought a live creature to cook before, except for the occasional bag of quietly gapping mussels. I'm not sure how I'll feel about it.

My parents are back in London and Jeff is attending an exhibition in Chicago so Hannah and I have taken friends, Simon and Abigail, with us to Dorsoduro to help us explore and to hunt for crabs. It's always interesting to see Venice through other peoples' eyes, Simon is a photographer.

Carmini wakes me gently at 7.15 with its call-to-mass peal. Hannah sleeps through it. The hourly chime of bells connects me to a physical sense of time. I've thought of drawing a series of radiating circles on my map of Venice, one for each *campanile*, to show how far into the city you can hear each church's bells. It would resemble rain drops on a canal, hundreds of interconnecting radiating rings.

The slim, vertical view through the green wooden kitchen shutters reveals a bright day, blue sky and opal smooth canal. With an upward swishing sound I open the mosquito screen, push back the shutters, which clatter against the house, and peer out onto the canal. I'm hoping that, being early April, there will still be *moeche* in the market. These small green crabs eaten in various restaurants have fascinated me for years, and are the mysterious crabs with many names.

Our route weaves through Dorsoduro towards San Polo. Venetians from our *sestiere* are going to work on the other side of the Grand Canal, students walk to University. We follow a delivery man holding large trays of fresh warm rolls and loaves for restaurants and hotels. The wind coming up the *calle* wafts the heady aroma of freshly baked bread downstream of the cart to our thankful noses, we almost follow him beyond our turning. Shadows give us a bearing, but as the sky clouds over the sundial effect of the street vanishes and we lose our compass. Changing weather adds a new mask to each building. As well as altering texture and colour, rain unlocks and releases a unique set of Venetian scents and aromas, including the smell of the sea.

Venice has a careful, dishevelled and almost wilful sense of abandonment as it crumbles into the lagoon. Reminiscent of the abandoned cityscapes in the novels of JG Ballard, such as *The Drowned World*. A landscape on the edge of change, whose altered state reflects in the minds of its remaining inhabitants. Like the lagoon, expanding, contracting, always on the move, the city shifts as it decays. Venice is in a constant state of being rebuilt and fixed as it erodes, falling chip by chip into the sea, like a flaking cliff dropping archaeological fragments and fossils. Sometimes I feel that taking yet another photograph might cause more of its flaky magistery to drop into the canal, the incessant flash of tourists' cameras bleaching it out of existence.

At 10.30 the Pescheria is in full swing. Fortunately it's not an early-bird market, mid-morning still guarantees most items to be in stock if they're in season. Seen from outside, the long brightly lit catwalk-like stalls are piled high with fish, resembling a glistening Fabergé display. The FAO labels help tremendously as they not only tell me where the catch was caught but also provide the scientific names alongside the Italian. At a glance I can sidestep fish that have been air-freighted into the Mercato Ittico Il Tronchetto from every ocean under our sun. I don't come to the Rialto to eat Pacific prawns. The sad fact of a prawn's transatlantic journey is unfortunately lost as soon as it drops into a restaurateur's basket. The careful FAO labelling isn't transferred to menus, yet. Sadly the local fish are usually more expensive than those that have travelled thousands of miles. Our next trip should be back up the supply chain to the commercial market of Chioggia where dozens of trawlers are moored next to the church of San Domenico.

All the stalls are tended with great pride and a real passion for what they're selling. Hannah and Abigail peek around the bustling crowds at each stall looking for small dark crab. They're choosy, looking for lively crab. Their motives are different to mine as they want a couple of pet crabs to play with before releasing them into our canal. I want a fresh supper. The girls spot some trying to escape by walking over the surrounding *orate* and *branzino* (gilthead bream and sea bass). Nearby some *canocchie* (mantis shrimp) are flipping and scissor-kicking. Apparently they can take your finger off and have been known to break a glass aquarium. The girls point out some favourite crabs to the stall holder who grins widely. One hides under the FAO label.

I can see it's going to be hard to convince the girls that I want to cook the crabs later so I order a few spares. Hannah and Abigail share carrying the *moeche*, they name them Marco and Polo. In case the crab dishes aren't to everyone's liking I find the last pile of *latterini* (sand-smelts). I'm aware that I'm still avoiding the gaze of certain fish, boney fish, large tricky-to-cook fish. Waiting on the embarkation platform at Rialto for our homeward *vaporetto* a young German boy looks dumbstruck as Hannah and Abigail hold out their pet crabs, we offer to give him one, he's happy just looking. The rather bored pilot/driver of our *vaporetto* is reading *Casa Vacanza* in the wheel house as we saunter back up the canal. Back home, after they've had a quick photo-shoot, the few crabs I'm actually allowed to cook are dipped in beaten egg and popped in the fridge for later.

While the crabs marinate in the fridge we take turns with our fishing rod out of the kitchen window. I make a pair of stick-rods for those of us waiting a turn. We spend a quiet afternoon

fishing, I even have a go casting from the high terrace down into the canal below, avoiding the gondolas, like fishing off a cliff or a jetty. I return to cooking supper, but first Hannah and Abigail walk over the small bridge and find some slippery steps down to the water to release their clutch of crabs into the canal. I'm heartened that the girls do eat a few of the remaining delicious fried soft-shelled crabs for supper.

Later we go rat hunting in the dark streets, a rare treat. There can't be many cities one can feel so safe in walking about at night with young children. Abigail has pet rats in London so to spot a Venetian rat would be a holiday highlight, they're surprisingly hard to find. Crab catching can be equally low-tech out on the lagoon, an old method called *zapiega* or *sapega* (stamping with the foot) or *peca* (kicking, making a footprint) is sometimes used. A fisherman walks in a stretch of shallow lagoon at low tide, as he retraces his steps, crabs will have scuttled into some of the foot print impressions left by his boots. A less kind way to leave an impression on the lagoon is practised by the hydraulic dredging trawlers, the ones I saw from the airplane. They fish for clams. The action of these vessels continuously ploughs up the sediment, re-suspending it and settling again. The result is a gradual degradation of the lagoon, affecting the flora and fauna. It also re-disperses the chemicals laid down decades ago by agricultural run-off and industrial petrochemical pollution from Porto Marghera, which is like Venice's *The Picture of Dorian Gray*. A growing interest in fish makes any inquisitive cook think about the supply chain and in a city surrounded by water I'm particularly aware of water-borne pollution. Living here connects us on a domestic level. I watch the downpipe opposite as a washing machine empties its frothy water into the canal as someone's final spin comes to an end. I lean out and watch it seeping into the ecosystem below the kitchen window. We try to be as ecological as we can, knowing that it all ends up in the canal. Fortunately surveys of the lagoon show that the levels of many chemicals have been reduced and more is being done to try and clean up the lagoon, some of the fisheries here and in the Adriatic are using sustainable methods. We buy eco-labelled canned fish in the local Coop Italia which is a socially responsible supermarket that believes in locally-sourced quality food. They've stocked Friend of the Sea certified fish since 2004.

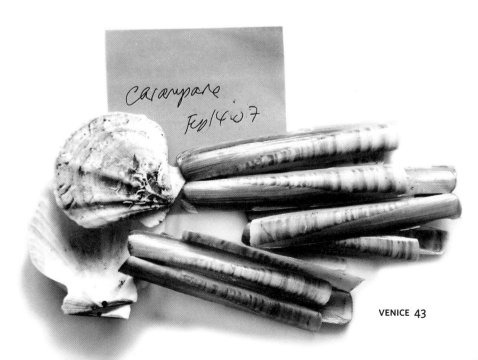

MOECHE FRITTE
FRIED SOFT-SHELL
SHORE CRAB

HANNAH AND ABIGAIL CHOSE ONE CRAB EACH AS PETS FOR THE DAY BEFORE RELEASING THEM INTO THE MURKY DEPTHS OF THE CANAL OUTSIDE OUR KITCHEN WINDOW. THEY'RE GIVEN NAMES; MARCO AND POLO, JEFFREY, AND THEN HUMPHREY, WHO BITES, AND HUMPY, WHO NIPS.

This dish is like delicate fishy scrambled eggs. It's worth visiting a Venetian kitchen in the autumn or spring just for these delicate flavoured soft-shell crabs, or to track them down in a restaurant. I'm not quite ready to cook large crabs or lobsters but this Venetian speciality allows me the opportunity to buy live crab and prepare them myself. The crabs are raised in captivity out on the lagoon so they can be taken to market when the shells are still soft. After buying the crabs we looked for cakes and cappuccinos. I became known as 2CakeJake after this visit.

SERVES 4

300g live soft-shell crabs, about 10 crabs
2 eggs
olive oil
5 tablespoons plain white flour
salt
lemon wedges

Wash the crabs well under running water, drain and place into a bowl.

Beat the eggs and add to the bowl of crabs. Put cling-film over the bowl and place it in the fridge for 1 hour. Stir the eggs and crab from time to time. The crabs will slowly ingest the egg.

Heat a wide frying pan, add olive oil, which only needs to be 5mm deep. Lightly dust the crabs in flour, a few at a time. Fry them in batches in the hot oil. Drain on paper towels.

Serve with salt and lemon and eat with hot runny white polenta.

SHORE CRAB

VENETIAN: Male – *granso, granso duro; granso bon* (nearing molting), *spiantano* (within a few days of moulting), *capeluo* (during molting), *moeca, moleche* (after molting), *strusso* (5–10 hours after molting but still saleable). Female – *masaneta, mazaneta* (with eggs), *masinetta, masina, masena. Granzi matti* or *falsi* are inedible hard crabs
ITALIAN: *Granchio commune*
SPECIES: *Carcinus mediterraneus* (Czerniavsky, 1884) and *Carcinus maenas* (Linnaeus, 1758)
FAMILY: *Portunidae* (Swimming Crabs)

Fishing of shore crabs in the lagoon occurs when the crabs make their new shells in the spring and autumn, and the pre-reproductive phase of female crabs in late summer-autumn. Spring crabs are supposed to taste the best. Carcinus maenas has been nominated as among the 100 of the 'World's Worst' invaders, finding itself in seas as far apart as South Africa, Australia, the Pacific and Atlantic North American coasts, and even in the entrance to Tokyo harbour.

Regione Veneto

FISHERMEN'S QUARTER

We've slowly become acquainted with our *sestiere*, Dorsoduro, feeling at home here, assisted by the fish tales of neighbours, architects, builders, artists and other friends in the city. Over the centuries fishing has helped shape our neighbourhood, it retains a small fish market in Campo Santa Margarita. Venice has been a destination-city for centuries, so thousands of maps, paintings and drawings help expand a picture of how the neighbourhood has changed. The paintings of JMW Turner show Dorsoduro of old, in 1840, with the beach of Santa Marta, lined with the huts and houses of poor fishermen, their fishing boats beached above the shoreline. The beach has since been replaced with the Stazione Marittima where the monumental cruise ships moor at the quayside. Like many other urban fishing communities this area was isolated and independent from the city. The fishermen were part of a workers' group calling themselves the *Nicolotti*, after San Nicolo the patron saint of sailors, merchants, archers, children, and students – the saint who eventually evolved into Santa Claus. The nearby fishermen's church of San Nicolò dei Mendicoli is the facade Donald Sutherland is restoring in the film *Don't Look Now*. It's an area that still retains working-class roots with houses built for railway workers in 1911 and new affordable housing added in the 1920s and 1930s. The university has taken over the old quayside warehouses adding student accommodation, so a youthful mix filters through the neighbourhood.

We don't get lost quite so often and Hannah navigates the complicated *calle* alone, happily venturing off to buy us fresh local shrimp or delectable little cakes. Shopping and cooking molluscs, fish and crustacea in this seafood-obsessed city has kick-started a growing passion for fish in us.

Venice has also pointed my exploration in a distinct and particular direction. I suspect that if I'd started this search in my local London supermarket many unexpected questions wouldn't have surfaced at all. Sadly Venice has also revealed that any city with such an iconic set of seafood dishes raises the expectations of visitors to demand them at any cost. This extreme demand has caused over-exploitation of local fish stocks. Only 20% of fish sold at the Rialto are caught locally. I wonder how many tourists unknowingly eat a plate of *calamari* in Venice that were actually caught in their hometown port thousands of miles away and air-freighted to Italy?

Leaving Venice by plane the slumbering city below resembles a giant monkfish, as if speared by the road-rail bridge to the mainland, spiked and caught. The plane banks gently, allowing us a farewell glimpse of the fyke nets and mussel farms of the northern lagoon.

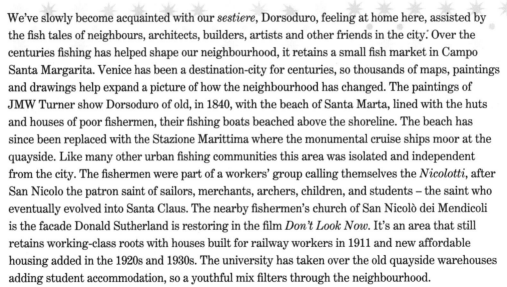

STANDING IN THE PESCHERIA AS A COOK HAS THROWN ME INTO THE LINGUISTIC DEEP END. WHY ARE FISH NAMES IMPORTANT? WHY DO THE UNITED NATIONS CARE? WHY ARE LOCALLY CAUGHT FISH SO HARD TO FIND? AND HOW WILL THESE QUESTIONS TRANSLATE WHEN ASKED ELSEWHERE? A CHANCE ANNIVERSARY INVITATION NEXT TAKES JEFF, HANNAH AND ME SOMEWHERE DEEPLY CONNECTED TO THE NAMING OF FISH – SWEDEN.

VIETATO
ACCOSTARE
Capitaneria di Porto
Comune di Venezia
Provveditorato al Porto

Fisk, fisk, fisk

Bohuslän, Sweden

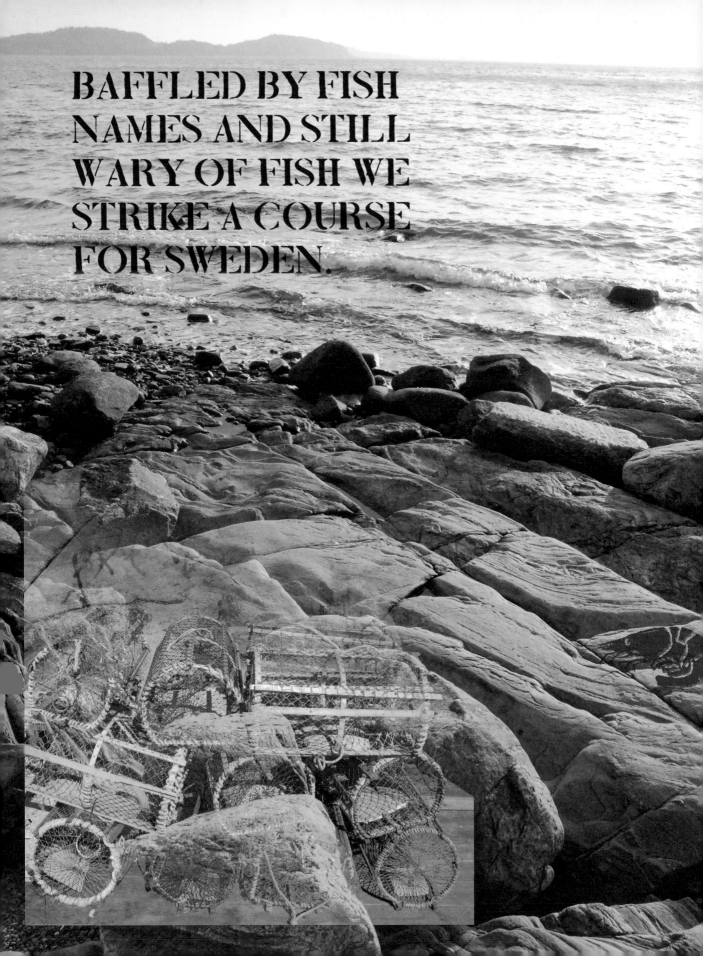

BAFFLED BY FISH
NAMES AND STILL
WARY OF FISH WE
STRIKE A COURSE
FOR SWEDEN.

IT WILL BE THE 300TH ANNIVERSARY OF THE BIRTH OF THE SWEDISH NATURALIST CARL LINNAEUS, WHO GAVE US MODERN TAXONOMY, THE SCIENCE OF CLASSIFYING ORGANISMS. WE HAVE AN INVITATION TO STAY WITH FRIENDS ON THE WEST COAST OF SWEDEN – A GREAT OPPORTUNITY TO EAT FISH AND HUNT FOR FISHERMEN'S COTTAGES.

VÄLKOMNA!

LINNÆUS

Working on my first cookbook, *A Tale of 12 Kitchens*, plunged me into the unfamiliar territory of recipe-writing and forced me to ponder their construction, grammar and complex system of rules. It was like trying to write poetry. Recipes for seafood require an altogether different order of organisation, more like a scientific dissertation. In Venice, when confronted with multiple names for the same fish and an ever-expanding list of sub-species to consider, taxonomy came to the rescue. Although not being a classicist means scientific names don't possess the same resonance for me as do the colloquial descriptions given to seafood. Carl Linnaeus unkindly named some of the uglier species after his worst critics. I prefer the nicknames that allow for local nuances and interests to emerge, as in the way Italians describe turbot, *rombo chiodato*. *Rombo* is used for many flat fish and *chiodato* means nailed or riveted, as a turbot resembles a nail-studded church door. I wonder whether sports fishermen have their own informal names for fish, dependant on how their catch are behaving – a hook-and-line dialect. With fish in mind, Carl Linnaeus's 300th birthday seems an apt occasion for a family visit to Sweden. Even before we arrive on Swedish soil I find a picture of Linnaeus on the 100 Kronor bank notes in my wallet – I'll use them to buy fish in Göteborg. I wonder if horticulturalists are visiting Sweden this year to make a similar linguistic pilgrimage?

One of the joys of staying with friends abroad is spending ridiculous amounts of time in their kitchens. Andie and Viktoria's long wooden clapboard house is outside Göteborg. On our first night, Jeff, Hannah and I receive ring-side seats to watch them prepare a seafood extravaganza. Huge *havskräfta* (Dublin Bay prawns), a basket of *nordhavsräka* (deep-water prawns), and *hälleflundra* (halibut) griddled gently and finished with white wine. Their cosy kitchen feels rather nautical, with slatted wood walls, painted off-white, and a ceiling that's 2 inches lower than I'd like. Viktoria is from the Ukraine, so some Russian dishes are planned. She has a natural curiosity about food and says that their finest meals are often prompted by those scary moments when you realise your guests are in their cars speeding towards your kitchen, and you haven't planned what to serve them. Look in the fridge, those will do, and suddenly a fabulous concoction is born. Many of Jeff and my more inventive meals occur when cooking just for each other. It becomes a culinary dialogue as we alternate who cooks from night to night, finding out which ingredients the other has left in the fridge, and whether leftovers remain uneaten or became a sandwich filling.

I don't think even Linnaeus could help identify the delicate little fish that Viktoria serves us as a starter. Miniature canned fish bought in Russia, called *ШПРОТ*, not a scientific name to be seen. It's strange to travel all the way to Sweden and be stumped by the first fish on a plate. Delicious little fish, but I want to know what they're called. That night I dream of fish names, not a *Carcharodon carcharias* in sight.

Hannah is up early and lets their cat Tolstij, Russian for fatso, into our room to help rouse us. Tolstij has a look of constant surprise on her pretty face, as if she's just seen a prawn. A portrait of Linnaeus peers up from the Sunday morning newspaper supplement. His classification of fish can be useful to untangle certain practices such as disguising strange fish by bestowing on them new names, a common ploy to lure us away from our stubborn seafood eating habits. The fish industry call this 'species substitution'. Eventually these names slip into common usage, such as monkfish, once confusingly known as scampi. Our local Chinese restaurant recommends St Peter's fish, I imagine it will be John Dory (San Pietro) or maybe tilapia (sometimes called St Peter's fish); of course it ends up being carp. Fish linguistics can be confusing, I have to learn a new language, a type of aquatic Esperanto. Some languages have different names for the same fish depending on whether it's alive or cooked, rather like pig and pork. As I found in Venice, gastronomy adds another layer of names, taking taxonomy into the kitchen. Here in Sweden further ambiguity is added to fish when they are given product names, after being canned, smoked or made into fish-paste.

Today we're off to church, Feskekôrka, the fish church. We set out across flat lands. Dark earth, enigmatic villages, desolate truck stops. Miniature two-person bus shelters look as if they have been dropped from a space ship, maybe they're a public arts commission. I see a tall man stooping in one awaiting the Göteborg bus. Woodland of silver birch look like shimmering pink feathers stuck into earth. Elsewhere there's a faint green haze, leaves ready to burst forth, crops baring tentative shoots to the cold spring air.

Feskekôrka is an indoor seafood market in Göteborg for local cooks and chefs alike. The impressive brick exterior squatting next to the cold rippling waters of the Rosenlund canal resembles a semi-submerged gothic barn. Inside the church-like interior we gaze at immaculate displays of northern seafood, a different palette of colours to those of the Mediterranean. As I slowly displace my fear of fish I'm beginning to get an eye for freshness. The advice I've read seems simple: fish should smell of the sea, not of fish. If they smell too fishy they're already old. The flesh should be firm and springy to touch. Fish should be slippery with stiff tails. Eyes should be clear, not cloudy and the blood in the gills should be bright red. That's it. It does take practice to notice these details, and perhaps you need to experience really fresh fish to see what you've been missing. When a fish is filleted however some of those telltale signs aren't there to test, fillets should be white and translucent. Beyond freshness there is also the state of the fish, determined by how well they were caught. Are they unscathed or battered about? Positioned next to the North Sea with the Atlantic beyond, the sense of what's local in this market encompasses a larger expanse of sea than in Venice. All of the produce here was fished in the North Atlantic or the North Sea. The king crab are huge, with legs the size of a human arm. *Torsk* (cod), *havskatt* (wolf-fish), *lax* (salmon), *sill* (herring), *blåmussla* (mussels), *sandmussla* (soft-shelled clams), *ostron* (oysters). Surprisingly I don't feel that connection to the sea I sense when standing in a Mediterranean fish market, maybe it's the modern additions of chilled cabinets, screens and mirrors which overpower the ancient interior of this barn. Once there used to be tanks full of live fish here, and the surrounding quayside was densely packed with pubs and cafes and the canal had a double row of fishing shacks. Their only neighbour today is a towering tax office.

FÄRSKA RÄKOR

V. QVIRIST EFTR.
Tel. 031 - 711 51 89, 13 46 81

FESKEKÔRKA

FESKEKÔRKA

Jansson's temptation

Abundance of any natural ingredient prompts invention and in Sweden many of these marine wonders end up canned. We find Swedish cured anchovies in the chilled section of supermarkets, and recognize them from back home at IKEA! You'll need to find a Swedish food stockist as they are NOT really anchovies, they're sprats. This classic Swedish dish uses them to great effect. As Jane Grigson says in her book *Fish* 'don't use milk instead of cream… as the beauty of the title will escape you.' Perhaps just eat it once a year. The anchovies are sweet and slightly spiced.

SERVES 4

sunflower oil

2 large white onions, thinly sliced

800g potatoes, peeled and cut into matchsticks

2 x 100g tins Swedish anchovy-style sprat fillets

black pepper

200ml double cream

125ml milk

70g white breadcrumbs

60g unsalted butter

Preheat the oven to 230°C/ Gas Mark 8.

Saute the onions in a little butter or sunflower oil until translucent.

Butter an ovenproof dish. Put in a layer of potato strips, then the sprat fillets and cover with the cooked onions, remaining potatoes and black pepper. Pour in a little of the oil from the canned fish (not too much, as it's surprisingly strong).

Heat the cream and milk in a pan until hot, but not boiling. Pour over the potatoes and fish. Spread the breadcrumbs over the top and dot with butter. Bake for 10 minutes, then reduce to 200°C/ Gas Mark 6 and cook for a further 45 minutes, until the potatoes are tender and the topping is crisp.

SPRAT

SWEDISH: *Skarpsill, vassbuck, aptitsill*
COMMON NAMES: *Sprat, whitebait (small sprat or herring)*
SPECIES: *Sprattus sprattus (Linnaeus, 1758)*
FAMILY: *Clupeidae (Herrings, Shads, Sardines, Menhadens)*

Ansjovis are cured in a spicy brine with cinnamon, sandalwood and ginger and taste rather sweet. Curiously *ansjovis* means 'anchovy' in Swedish, why am I not surprised! Sometimes called 'anchovy-style' sprats – equally confusing. They even make their way into anchovy paste.

Janssons Frestelse

Ansjovisbollar
Anchovy balls

SPRAT
SEE: *page 56*

Having tracked down *Svensk ansjovis* (Swedish anchovy-style sprat fillets) at IKEA and at two shops in London: Totally Swedish and Scandinavian Kitchen, I sought out other recipes that use these delicious sweet fish. They are the only canned fish I've found in the cold section of a shop.

SERVES 3

200g Swedish anchovy-style sprat fillets

2 eggs, hard-boiled

a dash of Worcestershire sauce

50g butter at room temperature

8 tablespoons finely chopped flat-leaf parsley

In a bowl, mash together the sprats, eggs, Worcestershire sauce and butter. Using a pair of teaspoons form the mixture into small ball-sized heaps and drop them onto a plate. Refrigerate for an hour or so, until set.

Once set, form into balls and roll in chopped parsley before serving as an appetizer or as a sandwich filling.

Fågelbo - Bird's nest

SERVES 1

4 Swedish anchovy-style sprat fillets, finely chopped

1 tablespoon finely chopped white onion

1 tablespoon capers, drained, washed, dried and chopped

2 tablespoons finely chopped pickled beetroot

1 tablespoon finely chopped flat-leaf parsley

1 egg yolk

Carefully arrange all of the ingredients round the edge of a serving dish except the egg yolk, which you place in the middle of the dish.

At table stir the ingredients together with the egg. Serve.

Variation
Either crumble a hard-boiled egg in the middle or use a fried egg for a great Sunday brunch.

Gravadlax

I'm nervous to include recipes for salmon as it's a fish that is so over-used but you only need a few thin slices of gravadlax to enjoy it. Alternatively it's a great recipe for other species of fish.

Gravadlax reminds me of another Swedish seafood delicacy, *surströmming*, which is soured, fermented herring. It smells of rotten eggs but tastes remarkably delicate and sweet. Some airlines forbid the transportation of *surströmming*, worried that the bulging, fermenting cans will explode onboard. Alan Davidson recalls that on the island of Ulvön when 200 barrels of *surströmming* were opened birds fell out of the sky dead. Unlike *surströmming* gravadlax is no longer fermented and is instead made using a dry marinade and refrigeration.

This is so easy to make and is meltingly delicious. Most coastal communities have developed their own strange and wonderful ways to preserve fish. With the advent of refrigeration these techniques are no longer needed, but we so love the taste of cured, smoked and pickled things many old methods are still in use. Sweden is obsessed with curing fish with sweet, spicy, herby mixtures. *Grav* means 'grave', or hole in the ground, or dig. In the Middle Ages the salmon were salted and buried in sand to ferment. These days a dry cure is used. As the British cook Hugh Fearnley-Whittingstall suggests, this recipe can also be made with mackerel or sea trout.

SERVES 6 AS A STARTER

550g wild or organic farmed salmon, cut as 2 matching fillets, pin-boned and skin on

Cure

1 tablespoon black or white pepper

3 cloves, crushed

2 tablespoons sea salt

2 tablespoons white caster sugar

75g dill, roughly chopped

Mustard and dill sauce

25g Dijon mustard

25g wholegrain mustard

1 tablespoon clear honey or white sugar

1 teaspoon white wine vinegar

1 teaspoon sunflower oil

2 tablespoons finely chopped dill

To make the cure, mix the pepper, cloves, salt, sugar and dill together in a bowl.

Choose a shallow dish the size of one fillet. Place a wide piece of cling film inside the dish overlapping each side. Take a quarter of the cure mix and make a fillet-sized bed of it on the cling film, then put on a salmon fillet skin-side down. Cover the fillet with half of the remaining cure and then the second fillet skin-side up, making a sandwich. Cover with the last of the mix. Wrap the clingfilm over and under the sandwiched fillets, tucking in the ends.

Put a piece of wood or a small tray on top of the parcelled fish and weigh it down with heavy jars or a brick. Compressing the fish helps the cure and will make the flesh denser and easier to slice. Refrigerate, turning the fish parcel once a day for five days.

Make the mustard and dill sauce an hour or so before serving the fish. Mix all the ingredients together in a bottle or jar and shake well.

Take out the fish, pour off the brine that has formed and wipe off some of the cure leaving the dill. Place the fish skin-side down and slice it not too thinly at a slight angle, leaving a layer of dill on each slice. Discard the skin. Serve with buttered brown bread and the mustard and dill sauce.

Unsliced leftovers should be drained of any brine and can be stored in the fridge for up to five days.

Fish in a Fur Coat

IF I HADN'T WATCHED VIKTORIA MAKE SHUBA I WOULD HAVE THOUGHT IT WAS SOMEONE'S BIRTHDAY AND WE WERE ABOUT TO EAT A LUSCIOUS LOOKING CHERRY CAKE, OR A RASPBERRY TRIFLE.

I'll definitely use this recipe when I next have fresh beetroot from my allotment, we're always looking for new ways to use the surplus. *Shuba* means fur coat in Russian. I'm not sure whether this is because of the way the dish is constructed or how satisfying it is to eat. The Russian name is *selyodka pod shouboy*, herring under fur coat. *Or salat shuba*, fish in a fur coat. Either way it's a glorious way to eat beetroot and herring.

SERVES 4

500g potatoes
140g carrots
300g beetroot
3 large free range eggs, hard boiled

280g soused or pickled herring fillets, de-boned and sliced
1 small red onion, finely sliced into rings
100g mayonnaise

Boil the potatoes, carrots and beetroot until cooked, leave them all to cool. Peel the beetroot once cool.

Grate the cold potato and beetroot onto separate plates. Chop the carrots. Crumble the hard boiled eggs.

Assemble the dish on a round plate or in a terrine dish to make it look like a layer cake. First arrange a layer of herring, then onion rings and grated potato. Spread on half the mayonnaise. Next add a layer of beetroot, then carrot. Spread on the remaining mayonnaise. Finally top with the crumbled egg. Leave in a fridge for at least an hour or better still, overnight.

Variations

Some people grate raw beetroot and then steam it for 15 minutes. It's also good with smoked salmon instead of herring. There are many variations on how to layer the mixture. If you have a more vertical stack you might want to alternate layers so that they remain thin, like *mille feuille*.

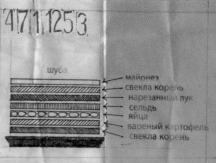

Shuba

Fish Smoke

Before heading back up the coast we need to buy something for supper. Joining the traffic flowing out of the city we pass the vast Stena Link car ferries, oil tankers and cargo container vessels in the port. Eventually we enter a development of commercial warehousing and car dealerships lined with flowing flags as if poised for a cavalry charge. Ahead of us Andie points out a tall, narrow chimney which is billowing pale smoke against a woodland backdrop, it's the fish smokery at Tagene. The single-storey building made from blue and white ribbed steel could be anything, although sea-inspired parking bollards provide a clue. We're in luck, they're still open. Inside the metal swing doors is a shop full of smoky wonders, resembling the vault of a gold bullion exchange. A chilled counter displays ingots of hot-smoked *lax*, whole smoked *ål* (eels), trays of smoked *sill*, *makrill* (mackerel), *hälleflundra* and lake fish. Choosing what to buy is hard so we ask the owner who is busy behind the counter for advice. Once he sees our inquisitiveness he kindly invites us back into the smoke room to see what's in production.

He's extremely friendly and proud of his smoked fish. We file through into a long slippery room covered in 1970s decorative tiles and a row of tall metal doors with heavy hinges. He unlatches one. The inside looks like a nocturnal rainforest exhibit, pale creatures hang from thin branches – they're actually rows of skewered *sill* fillets. Small logs burn gently at the base of this blackened cupboard, drying out the fish for a few hours, after which sawdust is added and the smoking begins. The next chimney is packed with racks of whole *lax*, each two feet long. Opening another submarine-like door a dense wall of smoke explodes outwards from all points, billowing and rolling into the room, causing us all to cough. He pulls out a cage of fish, deftly rotates it and slides it back in for further smoking. Racks of *hälleflundra* steaks wait their turn, as does a cage of small lake fish from Vantern. The owner recently smoked a huge 3 kilo *ål* caught on the east coast. His supplies come directly from a few fishing boats he knows well and trusts. In another series of rooms *torsk* are salted and then dried on a long ladder beneath a huge wind machine. Back in the shop we buy a whole hot-smoked *lax* for supper. The smoke-hardened skin, like golden armour, keeps in the extraordinarily delicate flavour of the pink flesh. Andie buys kippers, smoked *makrill* and a boned smoked *lax*, which consists of two large fillets lashed together with string mesh. It's all too fresh to vacuum pack, so we stow away our booty carefully into an air-tight container.

By the time we reach home the shadows are turning blue. It's still light outside as we gather the smoky components for supper. Viktoria has made thick pancakes using buckwheat flour, milk, live yeast, sugar and cornflower oil – cooked first side quite long, second side briefly. We sample the smoked fish before, during and after supper. It changes flavour with each tasting, shifting between moist and smoky. The pancakes are smothered with Ukrainian cods' roe and sour cream, the perfect fuel for tomorrow as we plan a dawn visit to the commercial fish market in town, the Fiskhamn.

Sprat stack

BALTIC SPRAT

SWEDISH: *Europeisk skarpsill, skarpsill, vassbuck, aptitsill*

COMMON NAMES: *Sprat, brisling, whitebait (small sprat or herring), garvie, garvock*

SPECIES: *Sprattus sprattus balticus* (Schneider, 1908)

FAMILY: *Clupeidae (Herrings, Shads, Sardines, Menhadens)*

Sprats are fast-growing and short-lived, which makes them less prone to overfishing. We found many canned sprat products in Swedish supermarkets. Amongst the most popular is *sardiner*, brisling, which are smoked and canned in oil or tomato sauce.

Viktoria prepared these beautiful, dainty tasty starters from a precious can of miniature ШПРОТ. To identify this fish I consult a book that Linnaeus would have loved, *The Multilingual Dictionary of Fish and Fish Products*. This esoteric book began life in the 1960s at the Torry Research Station in Aberdeen. The book even has a Russian index, which informs me that the small canned fish are brisling (small sprats). They're caught and sometimes farmed in the Baltic Sea, where the water is so brackish that freshwater fish can be caught out on the open sea. Frying grated carrot seems a surprising suggestion but tastes extremely good. Andie and Viktoria give me two more cans to take home! What friends! The fish are so small and delicate they look as if they've been shrunk – they taste delicious.

SERVES 6

2 aubergines, sliced into 12 thin rounds

sunflower oil

3 carrots, coarsely grated

3 cloves garlic, crushed

3 tablespoons mayonnaise

20 ШПРОТ, small canned brisling, reserving the oil from the can

Fry or griddle the aubergine slices in as little sunflower oil as you can get away with. Remove when browned.

Add the grated carrot to the pan and fry in a little sunflower oil until the carrot has wilted but retains some crunch. Remove to a bowl. Once the carrot has cooled, stir in the garlic and mayonnaise.

To assemble your sprat stacks: start with a slice of aubergine, add a spoonful of the carrot mix and cover with another slice of aubergine. Top this with three or four brisling and drizzle with a little of the oil from the canned fish.

Fiskbullar Fishballs

These fishballs are light in texture, slightly spongey, rich and tasty. They are glorious with the velvet smooth lemon sauce opposite. I make them with coley or pouting, both of which are inexpensive white fish perfect for fishballs.

MAKES ABOUT 20 FISHBALLS

1 large coley/pouting fillet, 500g, pin-boned and skinned

50g butter

salt and pepper

2 egg yolks

3 tablespoons single cream, or sour cream

2 egg whites

600ml fish stock

Make sure the fillet is completely free from bones. Roughly chop up the fillet and add to a food processor with the butter and seasoning. Blend until smooth. Turn into a bowl and mix in the egg yolks and cream.

In another bowl beat the egg whites until stiff, then gently fold into the fish mix.

Bring the stock to a boil in a wide pan. Reduce to a simmer.

With the aid of two tablespoons take some of the fish mixture and form into a 3cm ball, about the size of a large marble, and lower this gently into the simmering stock. Continue adding fishballs until the pan is full. Cook for 10 minutes. You may need to do two batches as the fish balls expand slightly during cooking.

When cooked, remove with a slotted spoon and keep warm until serving.

Fishballs 2

This makes a fish-only ball, no egg, which works nicely in fish stew as it's slightly more robust. These fishballs could also be made into flat patties and fried, or brushed with olive oil and baked. If the fillets are fresh these fishballs would be good left uncooked and frozen for cooking another day.

MAKES ABOUT 10 FISHBALLS

250g coley or pouting, pin-boned, skinned and chopped

2 teaspoons finely chopped chervil

salt and pepper

600ml fish or chicken stock

Place all the ingredients except the stock in a food processor and whiz briefly to a coarse paste. Turn out into a bowl and refrigerate for an hour.

Form the fish mix into a plateful of small fishballs as above. Poach in fish or chicken stock for 10 minutes. Remove with a slotted spoon.

COLEY

SWEDISH: *Gråsej, sej*
COMMON NAMES: *Saithe, coalfish, glassan, gloshan, sillock, billet, American pollock*
SPECIES: *Pollachius virens (Linnaeus, 1758)*
FAMILY: *Gadidae (Cod)*

Coley is similar to cod in texture: white, flakey and firm.

POUTING

SWEDISH: *Skäggtorsk*
COMMON NAMES: *Bib, pout, pout whiting*
SPECIES: *Trisopterus luscus (Linnaeus, 1758)*
FAMILY: *Gadidae (Cod)*

Pouting has the benefit of being relatively fast-growing and has a shorter lifespan than cod, of which it's a close relative.

Fiskbullsgryta
Fishball Stew

If you cook more fishballs than you need or have some frozen, here are two recipes that use them.

SERVES 3

1 stick celery, chopped
1 clove garlic, chopped
1 white onion, chopped
olive oil
2 x 400g cans chopped tomatoes

80g fresh or frozen peas
salt and pepper
12 fishballs (recipe opposite)

In a large pan, saute the celery, garlic and onion in a little olive oil until translucent.

Add the chopped tomatoes and season with salt and pepper. Simmer for 15 minutes, adding a little water if it gets dry. Use a potato masher to gently squash down the tomatoes, breaking them apart.

Add the peas and fishballs and simmer for 15 minutes, or until cooked through.

Bakade Fiskbullar - Baked Fishballs

SERVES 3

15 fishballs (recipe opposite)
150g leaf spinach
60g breadcrumbs
1 tablespoon butter, optional

Citronsås *(lemon sauce)*
40g butter
2 tablespoons plain white flour
300ml stock (chicken, fish, veg)
100ml milk
juice of 1 lemon and ½ grated rind
1 egg yolk

To make the *citronsås* (lemon sauce), melt the butter in a small pan, add the flour, and cook, stirring, a minute or two. Gradually add the stock, stirring out any lumps and cook for a further 5 minutes. Add the milk, lemon juice and rind and simmer for a few minutes without boiling. Beat the egg yolk in a cup and stir it quickly into the sauce, stirring continuously for 3 minutes, without boiling.

Preheat the oven 220°C/ Gas Mark 7. In a small oven dish that can take the fishballs in one layer, arrange a deep bed of spinach leaves. Place the fish balls on top, pushing them slightly into the spinach. Pour over a good covering of lemon sauce, topping it with breadcrumbs. Add a few dabs of butter if you like. Bake for 20 minutes until crispy on top. Serve with new potatoes. Use any spare lemon sauce on white fish fillets.

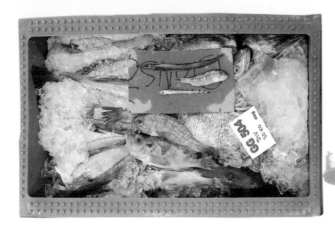

GÖTEBORGS
FISKHAMN

Sigvard Fotö Blandat

FISKHA

Catch the Early Prawn

Darkness outside. Once dressed we test the air before making final clothing adjustments and witness the dawn beginning to illuminate the pale vista beyond the church. After a quick cup of green tea Andie, Jeff, Hannah and I slump tired into Andie's car. We enter a completely motionless landscape, our headlight beams strike out into the fog like a pair of detectives' torches seeking evidence. The E6 motorway is quiet until the dusky industrial outskirts of Göteborg, whose factories, depots and quaysides are gradually stirring. In theory Andie and Viktoria's house is on the North Sea coast, but with so much water about where's the sea? Being so far into the archipelago and network of inlets the sea here is non-tidal. We drive inland, a relative term here in Bohuslän. This motorway leads to Norway but the traffic is remarkably light, the entire population of Sweden is less than London's. Our route winds through endless forests and crosses many rivers. The shoreline seems to be on our left, then on our right, underneath us and then on both sides. As the navigator looking at the map, my sense of this porous landscape is altered by hundreds of small lakes that erode the green areas, leading east to the vast, glassy expanse of Lake Vänern. It's a coastline we travel through and over rather than along.

Eventually we reach the spiral ramp leading down to the Fiskhamn, the commercial fish market, before sunlight touches the tip of a forty-nine metre stone column on which sits a sculpture of the grieving mariner's wife, or mother, looking out across the Gota Canal and the fish market below. Refrigerated trucks and fish merchants bustle outside the auction hall, flanked by a small car park. Many fish markets have become tourist destinations, they're the closest most of us get to meeting a whole fish. There are no other visitors today. An auction hall is rather intimidating for a group that looks more like a family outing, we're definitely not seafood merchants. We take a tentative look around. Under the shallow pitched roof are neatly arranged rows of green or pale blue plastic crates. It's extraordinarily cold so the fish are in pristine condition. Andie and I inspect every row, walking up and down each aisle as if we're in a supermarket. The largest fish are *torsk* and the smallest we find is a diminutive *makrillgädda* (needlefish). I wonder how far afield these fish might now travel? The auction bell rings, shaking a fish silhouette on top. Auctions break out at each end of the hall, merchants stand in small groups quietly buying boxes of fish. I'd been expecting the auction to be more theatrical, more overtly an auction, but they obviously don't require added antics to help sell fish here. Hannah and Jeff are chilled to the bone so retire to the car for some warmth.

Standing here facing these boxes of cod I have one of those pivotal moments, a shifting in perception, it almost feels like a panic attack. It was researching the naming of fish that opened the Pandora's box of overfishing for me. Part of learning about and loving fish requires accepting some bitter facts, if only to be able to step forward. Anyone who is passionate about food sooner or later needs to know where it comes from. Ironically it was the back of a menu in a fish and chip shop, The Seacow, that first drew my attention to a list of fish that one shouldn't eat because of overfishing. Overfishing causes a species to lose the ability to reproduce by unbalancing the age range within a fish community, or by reducing its mass below a point where it collapses and can't recover. Catching too many young fish is known as growth overfishing, a particular problem for bottom-dwelling, demersal fish such as cod, who only begin to breed when they're 2 or 4 years old. There are virtually no cod in the North Sea older than 4. Catching too many large, sexually mature fish is called recruitment overfishing, a particular problem for non-bottom-dwelling, pelagic fish such as herring or anchovy. The FAO, The Food and Agricultural Organisation of the

UN, report that 80% of the world's fish are over-fished. To compound overfishing there are two further evils created by the convergence of industrialised commercial fishing and politics, bycatch and discards. Bycatch is everything else that is caught while a boat is trying to catch a particular species. Many of the rules handed out to fishermen encourage or even reward what is now considered bad practice. Some bycatch is taken back to port if it's valuable, most is thrown back into the sea, dead. As well as 'non-targeted' fish, bycatch can include turtles, sharks, sea birds, bits of coral and other marine mammals. Fish are also discarded for economic or legislative reasons particularly in mixed, demersal (bottom-dwelling) fisheries where several species overlap. Why it occurs is extremely complicated and varies for each type of fishing. The fish caught may be over-quota, by-catch, or a fish that has no market value at all, so overboard they go. Many quotas are for a given weight of one species on one day – a stupid idea, as if you catch more on your first haul you have to throw away the difference. And if your first haul isn't valuable at the market you're also able to throw it away and re-shoot your nets for something more profitable to make the most of your permitted days at sea and pay for fuel and wages. Certain prawn fisheries, where 1 kilo of prawns landed requires 10 kilos of other fish being thrown overboard are notorious for waste. The statistics are numbing and sometimes contradictory, the FAO reports that 8% of the world's catch is discarded, whereas a recent World Wildlife Fund survey concludes that if you consider 'bycatch is catch that is either unused or unmanaged' this figure increases to 40%. As these facts sink in I feel as if I've entered a black hole, yet fortunately us consumers are a powerful force and we all have the chance to reverse this process, while continuing to eat fish. There are always exceptions to bad fishing practices – entire fisheries in Iceland have rules whereby everything that is caught is landed and discarding fish overboard is banned, this should be made law elsewhere.

Stepping back outside through the automated doors we almost feel warm, it's a seriously cold morning. Later we take a short tram ride up to the Sjöfartsmuseet, the Maritime Museum, next to the sailors' church, with views over the harbour, the fish market and copper-topped apartment blocks. The fishing industry quietly permeates this part of the city. Inside the Sjöfartsmuseet is reminiscent of many municipal museums, a faded elegance that hasn't been re-branded yet. An entire floor is dominated by ocean liners, seafaring and warfare, a reminder of other reasons for going to sea than fishing. On the third floor is an exhibition, 'Fishing on the West Coast of Sweden'. Large glass cabinets house dioramas demonstrating various trawling techniques in miniature. A thin glass sea is dotted with model trawlers, small seine nets below. I think some holographic herring are needed. A trawler wheelhouse sits in the middle of the room as does a huge hose that is used to suck out the catch from a trawler's holding tank onto the quayside. I wonder if local fishermen bring their children here and if it helps them to understand the gruelling job their parents do night and day out at sea.

Outside the rattling blue trams are saturated with spring sunshine, the perfect antidote to dark winter months. Passing by the Universeum (natural and physical sciences museum) we wander inside, hoping that their aquarium might contain some native fish. A few flat fish and lobsters swim restfully in a North Sea tank but I then turn a corner and find myself in the middle of Göteborg face to face with the pre-historic stare of a three metre long *sandtigerhajen*, sand tiger shark. Hannah thinks my fear of it is rather hysterical. I take out my video camera, putting something else between me and it. When back in my London studio I stumble again on this very same landlocked shark, courtesy of the Universeum Oceantank webcam, I can watch it live. Even

SMÖGENS FISKAUKTION

Köpare **53141**   03/04/2007
LL425   08:04   6 Lot: 4.001

SM-ERNSTS

Kokräkor 141-160 st/
< Må   2   30   KG

LEKSAKSBODEN

STINAS

KUNGSHAMN

HUNNEBOSTRAND

BOVALLSTRAND

in pixellated form menace emanates from my computer screen. Although surprisingly, unlike the printed photographs which sparked my fear of fish, the rather hypnotic pixels from the webcam become less threatening. I discover that the shark is called Herman.

We've visited as many supermarkets and shops as possible in all the towns we've passed along the coast, hunting out the fish sections, fresh and canned. By now Hannah must have a rather strange view of Sweden. Our last day is spent digging in Andie and Viktoria's fridge for the profusion of fish Jeff and I have stashed away, including beautiful pink cans of sprats, herring, a smoked mackerel and a seriously large hot-smoked salmon. I also have two precious black cans of silver Russian fish from Viktoria. So there is much to experiment with in the kitchen on our return.

When landing and taking off from coastal airports these days Jeff and Hannah kindly offer me the window seat. I sit with camera poised. The view from the plane opens up the archipelago and we see the open sea and the Fiskhamn too. The swirling granite coastline north of Göteborg seems to be a mixture of the granite colours from across the North Sea in Scotland, as if crossing the expanse of water merges and compresses them together.

As I try to grapple with the huge unwieldy question of sustainability I wonder if my newly found love of seafood has come forty years too late. Luckily I remember that on that Seacow menu was a list of fish that we can eat and cook, species that are being fished within 'safe biological limits'. It will cut swathes through my seafood recipe books. I start annotating my Alan Davidson field guides, not only making notes about what I've eaten, but also crossing out what I shouldn't and why. I then circle new fish for investigation.

Orust

NORWAY ↑

BOHUSLAN

E6

fishing huts
Bovallstrand
Sotenas
Munkedal
slow road
Uddevalla
Stangenas
ogen
Fiskhamn
awns
Bokenas
Henan
Ice cream
varekil
Tjörn
Stenungsund

N

Thursday 12th April

WE HAVE RETURNED HOME WITH A SET
OF SHARP FISH FILLETING KNIVES BOUGHT
AT THE GÖTEBORG CASH AND CARRY,
AND LEARNT SOME NEW KITCHEN SKILLS
INCLUDING HOW TO SPOT FRESH FISH.
SWEDEN SHARES THE NORTH SEA WITH
MANY NATIONS, INCLUDING SCOTLAND,
WHERE MY WIFE JEFF WAS BORN. I WONDER
HOW THEY COOK FISH IN ABERDEEN?

YE'LL BE HERE FOR THE FISH THEN?

ABERDEENSHIRE
SCOTLAND

LATITUDE 57 STRIKES OUT
FROM SWEDEN ACROSS THE
NORTH SEA, LANDING UPON
THE CRAGGY SHORELINE OF
ABERDEENSHIRE. TOWNS
AND LANDSCAPES SCULPTED
BY FISHING AND THE SEA.

THE WINDSWEPT PENINSULA JUTTING OUT INTO THE FOAMING WILDS
OF THE NORTH SEA IS WHERE MY WIFE'S FAMILY FARM SITS UPON AN
EXPOSED HILLSIDE. THIS AREA WAS DESCRIBED BY THE ANCIENT GAELS AS
'THE LAND AT THE BEND IN THE SEA'. I THOUGHT I WAS GETTING TO KNOW
ABERDEENSHIRE UNTIL I LOOKED AT MY FISH SUPPER AND WAS REMINDED
OF THE SEA.

The FISHING INDUSTRY in Aberdeen

THE ABERDEEN FISH MARKET PUBLICITY

COMMERCIAL QUAY

ABERDEEN HARBOUR BOARD

Tel. 01330 833462
Fax. 01330 833478

PARKING RESTRICTED
TO FISHMARKET USERS ONLY

main
light

berth
light

ABOARD THE ABERDEEN FISH

How you choose to arrive in a city shapes your first impressions of it, framing the moment and location like a series of establishing shots in a movie. A perfect passage to the granite city of Aberdeen, in North-East Scotland, is to take the overnight Caledonian Sleeper train from London Euston, leaving the dark empty station at 9.15pm. Travelling by rail sidesteps the crowded shopping-mall hell of airline terminals, misty with the smell of frying fat, hissing cappuccinos and a growing fear of flying. As airport architecture and its suburbs of arterial slip roads, freight warehouses and multi-storey car parks becomes more and more homogenous rail travel can still surprise. Trains take you deep into the heart of a city, emerging in a real neighbourhood – not a travelator or rattling luggage carousel in sight. As our Sleeper thunders north, Jeff, Hannah and I are taking the reverse route of the 'Aberdeen Fish', a train that brought fresh fish to London from Scotland until the 1960s. A long, stinking goods train which sprayed the railway tracks with cold, oily water coming off iced boxes of cod, mackerel and haddock. The dark sounds of our night train wake me in the small hours, like a sleepy horn ensemble of droning bassoons, syncopated with the rhythmic vibrations of the steel tracks.

On past visits to Scotland it's been family farming connections to the land that have formed my impressions of the gentle rolling hills and stone dyke-lined roads, and of Aberdeenshire's gastronomic culture. Landscapes I thought I knew well now appear hazy and indistinct. I must have been half asleep not to notice the profound effect the sea and fishing have had on this country. Several waves of industry are common to both Scandinavia and Scotland – both discovered North Sea oil and natural gas a month apart in 1969. They share a fishing history of whaling from 1788 to 1893 and herring from 1896, until overfishing wiped it out by 1960. Their fleets now catch white fish and prawns.

A sharp knock at 7am on our interlocking two-berth compartment door wakes us from our locomotive sleep. After a tea and shortbread breakfast I pull up the window blind to reveal a blurred Easter blue horizon on the North Sea. It's magical to fall asleep passing through the London suburbs and awaken by the sea – a sense of dislocation. Damp green fields dip and drop as ragged cliffs and coves reveal treacherous rocks below, crashing waves and white foaming spume. Morning is still unravelling as the grey sea is replaced by the stoical silver-grey granite of Aberdeen. We stow away our night gear and stumble blearily onto the empty platform. Jeff and Hannah walk briskly to catch a northbound Buchan bus to the farm, leaving me in Aberdeen. Being transported in my sleep to arrive at the crack of dawn within two minutes of a port and a commercial fish market is an exciting prospect. It's with a sense of exploration and not fear that I'm meeting a friend to go fishing on a small boat.

The early morning air is bitterly cold. Giant oil and gas supply vessels sit quietly in their deep-water berths in Upper Dock. Their brightly coloured towers and tall communication masts merge with the sandstone spires of St Andrew's Episcopal Cathedral and the pointed steeple and granite turrets of The Toon Hoose clock on Union Street. This composite view would have been similar a century ago, though cluttered instead with great tall-masted sailing ships. Aberdeen doesn't possess an equivalent public market to the Pescheria in Venice or the Feskekôrka in Göteborg – to help me map out what's caught and landed on this side of the North Sea I'll have to look elsewhere. As I endure the cold wind blowing off the harbour along a deserted Market

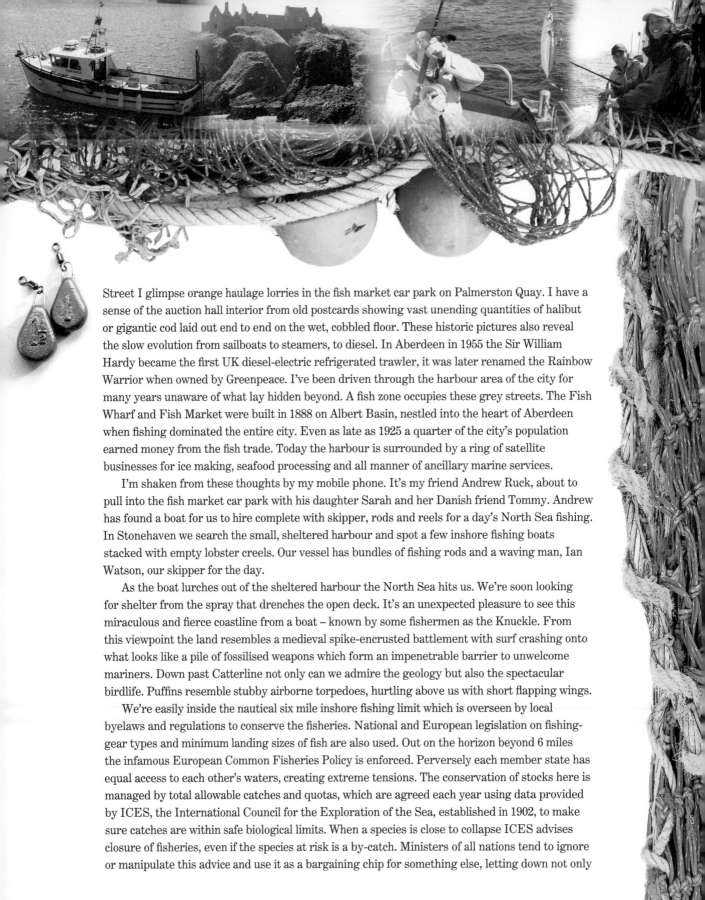

Street I glimpse orange haulage lorries in the fish market car park on Palmerston Quay. I have a sense of the auction hall interior from old postcards showing vast unending quantities of halibut or gigantic cod laid out end to end on the wet, cobbled floor. These historic pictures also reveal the slow evolution from sailboats to steamers, to diesel. In Aberdeen in 1955 the Sir William Hardy became the first UK diesel-electric refrigerated trawler, it was later renamed the Rainbow Warrior when owned by Greenpeace. I've been driven through the harbour area of the city for many years unaware of what lay hidden beyond. A fish zone occupies these grey streets. The Fish Wharf and Fish Market were built in 1888 on Albert Basin, nestled into the heart of Aberdeen when fishing dominated the entire city. Even as late as 1925 a quarter of the city's population earned money from the fish trade. Today the harbour is surrounded by a ring of satellite businesses for ice making, seafood processing and all manner of ancillary marine services.

I'm shaken from these thoughts by my mobile phone. It's my friend Andrew Ruck, about to pull into the fish market car park with his daughter Sarah and her Danish friend Tommy. Andrew has found a boat for us to hire complete with skipper, rods and reels for a day's North Sea fishing. In Stonehaven we search the small, sheltered harbour and spot a few inshore fishing boats stacked with empty lobster creels. Our vessel has bundles of fishing rods and a waving man, Ian Watson, our skipper for the day.

As the boat lurches out of the sheltered harbour the North Sea hits us. We're soon looking for shelter from the spray that drenches the open deck. It's an unexpected pleasure to see this miraculous and fierce coastline from a boat – known by some fishermen as the Knuckle. From this viewpoint the land resembles a medieval spike-encrusted battlement with surf crashing onto what looks like a pile of fossilised weapons which form an impenetrable barrier to unwelcome mariners. Down past Catterline not only can we admire the geology but also the spectacular birdlife. Puffins resemble stubby airborne torpedoes, hurtling above us with short flapping wings.

We're easily inside the nautical six mile inshore fishing limit which is overseen by local byelaws and regulations to conserve the fisheries. National and European legislation on fishing-gear types and minimum landing sizes of fish are also used. Out on the horizon beyond 6 miles the infamous European Common Fisheries Policy is enforced. Perversely each member state has equal access to each other's waters, creating extreme tensions. The conservation of stocks here is managed by total allowable catches and quotas, which are agreed each year using data provided by ICES, the International Council for the Exploration of the Sea, established in 1902, to make sure catches are within safe biological limits. When a species is close to collapse ICES advises closure of fisheries, even if the species at risk is a by-catch. Ministers of all nations tend to ignore or manipulate this advice and use it as a bargaining chip for something else, letting down not only

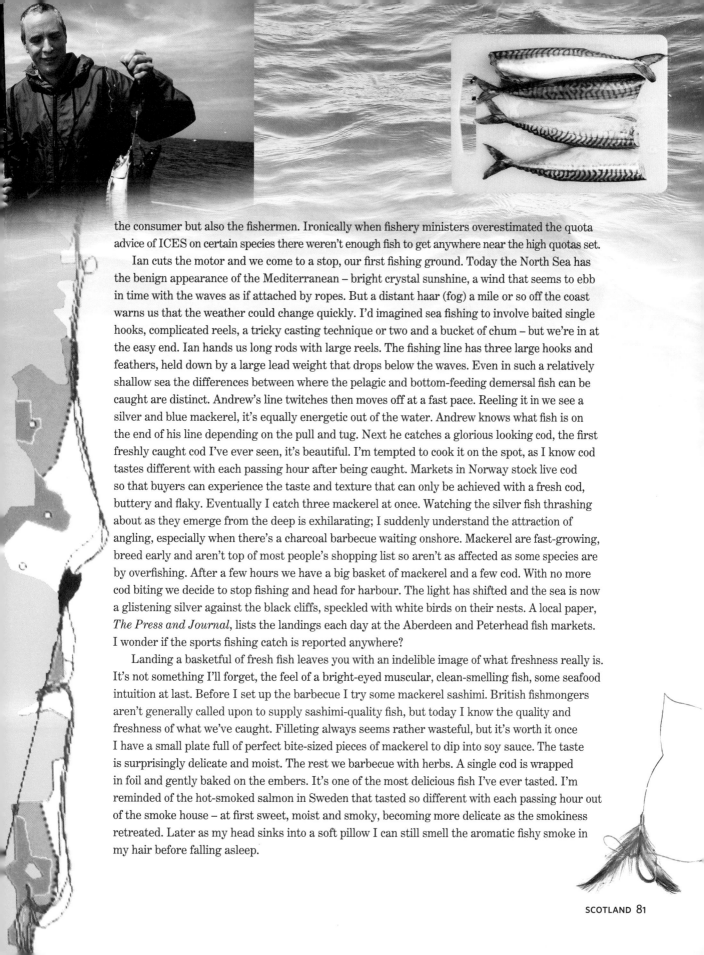

the consumer but also the fishermen. Ironically when fishery ministers overestimated the quota advice of ICES on certain species there weren't enough fish to get anywhere near the high quotas set.

Ian cuts the motor and we come to a stop, our first fishing ground. Today the North Sea has the benign appearance of the Mediterranean – bright crystal sunshine, a wind that seems to ebb in time with the waves as if attached by ropes. But a distant haar (fog) a mile or so off the coast warns us that the weather could change quickly. I'd imagined sea fishing to involve baited single hooks, complicated reels, a tricky casting technique or two and a bucket of chum – but we're in at the easy end. Ian hands us long rods with large reels. The fishing line has three large hooks and feathers, held down by a large lead weight that drops below the waves. Even in such a relatively shallow sea the differences between where the pelagic and bottom-feeding demersal fish can be caught are distinct. Andrew's line twitches then moves off at a fast pace. Reeling it in we see a silver and blue mackerel, it's equally energetic out of the water. Andrew knows what fish is on the end of his line depending on the pull and tug. Next he catches a glorious looking cod, the first freshly caught cod I've ever seen, it's beautiful. I'm tempted to cook it on the spot, as I know cod tastes different with each passing hour after being caught. Markets in Norway stock live cod so that buyers can experience the taste and texture that can only be achieved with a fresh cod, buttery and flaky. Eventually I catch three mackerel at once. Watching the silver fish thrashing about as they emerge from the deep is exhilarating; I suddenly understand the attraction of angling, especially when there's a charcoal barbecue waiting onshore. Mackerel are fast-growing, breed early and aren't top of most people's shopping list so aren't as affected as some species are by overfishing. After a few hours we have a big basket of mackerel and a few cod. With no more cod biting we decide to stop fishing and head for harbour. The light has shifted and the sea is now a glistening silver against the black cliffs, speckled with white birds on their nests. A local paper, *The Press and Journal*, lists the landings each day at the Aberdeen and Peterhead fish markets. I wonder if the sports fishing catch is reported anywhere?

Landing a basketful of fresh fish leaves you with an indelible image of what freshness really is. It's not something I'll forget, the feel of a bright-eyed muscular, clean-smelling fish, some seafood intuition at last. Before I set up the barbecue I try some mackerel sashimi. British fishmongers aren't generally called upon to supply sashimi-quality fish, but today I know the quality and freshness of what we've caught. Filleting always seems rather wasteful, but it's worth it once I have a small plate full of perfect bite-sized pieces of mackerel to dip into soy sauce. The taste is surprisingly delicate and moist. The rest we barbecue with herbs. A single cod is wrapped in foil and gently baked on the embers. It's one of the most delicious fish I've ever tasted. I'm reminded of the hot-smoked salmon in Sweden that tasted so different with each passing hour out of the smoke house – at first sweet, moist and smoky, becoming more delicate as the smokiness retreated. Later as my head sinks into a soft pillow I can still smell the aromatic fishy smoke in my hair before falling asleep.

3 FISH BAKE

This warming winter's dish is rather like an upside down potato and fish pie. It's enough for a whole meal and can be made with any white or smoked fish.

SERVES 3

175g leeks finely sliced

700g potatoes, cut into 1cm rounds

1 bay leaf

3 spring onions, chopped

salt and pepper

300ml milk

100ml water

200g haddock, skinless fillets

200g salmon, skinless fillets

100g smoked haddock

1 handful chopped chives

1 handful finely chopped flat-leaf parsley

Preheat the oven to 220°C/ Gas Mark 7.

In an oven-proof casserole dish, put the leeks, potatoes, bay leaf and spring onions and season with salt and pepper. Pour in the milk and enough water to barely cover the vegetables. Cook in the hot oven for 30 minutes, until browned.

Cut all of the fish into bite-sized pieces.

Remove the casserole from the oven. Mash a few of the cooked potatoes and mix them back into the stew.

Arrange the fish in a layer over the cooked vegetables. Sprinkle with chives and parsley. Add a little more milk if needed. Return to the oven and cook for a further 10-15 minutes, just long enough to cook the fish through. The stew should be bubbling up through the fish.

HADDOCK

COMMON NAMES: *Adag, attac, haddie, luckenar, nockie, Peterfish, pipe, poot, pout, rawn and roan*
Large: *Jumbo, gibber*
Medium: *Kit*
Small: *Calfie, chat, danny, norrie, pinger, powie, tiddley*
Very small: *Ping pong, seed*
SPECIES: *Melanogrammus aeglefinus (Linnaeus, 1758)*
FAMILY: *Gadidae (Cod)*

HADDOCK WRAP

One of the problems of being a recent fish-convert is that my seafood recipe library is small – not for long. Friends have recommended a cook from the 1970s, George Lassalle. I find a recipe of his that wraps a whole fish in bacon, using sea bream, haddock or codling. Today I have a few beautiful fresh haddock fillets off a Peterhead trawler, so I'll improvise. To emulate a whole fish I create a small stack of fillets. Some streaky bacon might help lard the fish, I have unsmoked back bacon so I'll add a touch of butter. The result is quick, easy and extremely succulent. If I were in Venice I might try prosciutto or sneak in a little pancetta.

SERVES 4

HADDOCK
SEE: *page* 82

4 small haddock fillets, skinned   *black pepper*
8 dabs of butter   *12 rashers unsmoked bacon*

Preheat the oven to 220°C/ Gas Mark 7.

Cut the fillets into 5 x 15 x 3cm pieces. Butter an oven dish. Slightly overlay three rashers of bacon, enough to cover a fillet. Lay one fillet piece across the bacon, dab it with butter, stack another fillet piece on top and dab with butter and pepper. Wrap the pieces of bacon over the fillet pieces. Repeat until you have one parcel per person.

Bake in the hot oven for 20 minutes. Good with new potatoes and a steaming pile of spinach or peas.

Commercial Quay

Albert Quay

KIPPERS AND CORN BBQ

HERRING
SEE: *pages* 60 & 93

KIPPERS
A kipper is a whole herring that has been split from tail to head, gutted, salted or pickled, and cold-smoked.

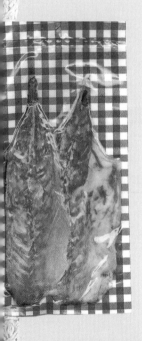

Wonderful, your garden fills with the smoky aromas rather than your kitchen. You can enjoy kippers without worrying that you're smoking your cookbooks. Cooked on a barbecue the small bones melt away, so can be eaten without too much worry.
SERVES 3

3 corn on the cob, halved lengthways
3 kippers, boned

Blanch the corn cobs in boiling water for 5 minutes, drain and keep warm.

Once your barbecue is ready, grill the corn cobs, they take longer than the fish.

Barbecue the kippers on a medium part of the grill for about 3 minutes each side.

KIPPER PATE

2 undyed kippers   *150g full-fat cream cheese*
2 teaspoons butter   *juice of 1 lemon*
½ teaspoon paprika   *fresh black pepper*
1 teaspoon horseradish

Preheat the grill. Dab the kippers with a little butter and cook skin side up gently for 1 minute, turn, then cook a further 4–5 minutes.

Alternatively try jugged kippers, this avoids kippering up your kitchen with fishy smells. Take off the heads, fold the splayed kipper together and place in tall jug. Fill with boiling water, cover with a lid and leave somewhere warm for 6 minutes or so. Drain and dry.

Once cooked (grilled or jugged), carefully remove the skin and bones with your fingers, feeling for any small bones.

In a food processor, add the deboned kipper flesh, paprika, prepared horseradish, cream cheese, lemon juice and pepper. Process just enough to make a coarse pate.

Refrigerate. Eat on hot buttered toast.

POTTED KIPPER

Cook the kippers as above, puree the deboned kipper flesh with the juice of 1 lemon and some cayenne pepper. Pack into a small dish, put on a few capers and cover with melted butter. Refrigerate. Eat on hot buttered toast.

SALMON PUDDING

It's Christmas and the supermarkets are all but bare. With a choice of farmed salmon or MSC-certified wild Alaskan salmon in the frozen section I go for the freezer – back at the farm we have some cold water Atlantic prawns in the fridge. This is based on an Eliza Acton recipe 'a Scotch receipt, good'.

SERVES 3

400g salmon fillets
100g white breadcrumbs
4 tablespoons double cream
3 eggs, whisked
salt and pepper
½ teaspoon paprika
200g cooked coldwater prawns

Poach the salmon in as little water as possible until barely cooked, about 5 minutes. Leave to cool.

Flake the salmon into a bowl, add the breadcrumbs, cream, eggs, salt, pepper and paprika and mix thoroughly. Refrigerate for 30 minutes.

Preheat the oven to 200°C/ Gas Mark 6.

Lightly butter an oven dish. Cover the base with a layer of prawns. Press the fish mixture on top, push any spare prawns into the mix.

Bake in the oven for 30 minutes. Eat hot or cold, with a salad.

Variation

For a more fishy, less solid pudding, add fewer breadcrumbs, only 2 eggs and don't use cream. Instead of prawns a layer of asparagus is good.

ATLANTIC SALMON

COMMON NAMES: *Black salmon, grilse, kelt, parr, sea salmon, silver salmon*
SPECIES: *Salmo salar, Linnaeus, 1758*
FAMILY: *Salmonidae (Salmon)*

Parr: Young salmon before it leaves fresh water.
Smolt: Young salmon, leaving fresh water for the sea.
Grilse: Salmon returning from the sea to fresh water having spent one winter at sea.
Kelt: Salmon that have spawned.

Organic farmed salmon is a reasonable alternative to wild as long as the farms become more accountable about where they source their fish feed from. Unlike wild salmon which have orange/pink flesh, farmed salmon naturally have pale flesh. Colour is added to the fish feed to make them orange. If I buy farmed salmon I look for pale, un-coloured, organic salmon, rather like buying smoked haddock that hasn't been dyed yellow.

FISHERTOUNS

The family farm is only eight miles from the breaking waves of the North Sea, the coast arches northwards dotted with small villages and a few hardy towns. Today we're going to Macduff, hopefully full of Scottish trawlers. Winter colours still cling to many plants and trees, the bare woodland allowing deep views scattered with wild daffodils and snowdrops that fizz in the ashen gloom. The meandering shape of the river Ythan winds across its flood plain like a drowsy adder hiding in tall reeds. Long shadows, short days. Buildings appear hunched against the wind, ear flaps down, coat collars up. An occasional copse of brave trees exposed on a hillside is permanently locked in a skewered position, bent and fixed by the wind. Suddenly there's the sea. As we enter Macduff and descend a steep hill the horizon rises like a giant tidal wave. It's a pretty town, despite the cold, and seen from the sea I imagine it becomes invisible, the slate roofs and granite walls stacked up the hillside, hiding like a stone chameleon. Berthed at high tide behind the safety of the harbour wall are a small fleet of trawlers. These vessels, rigged for crabbing with creels, seine netting, or trawling, all possess a singular purpose whose engineering is aimed at extreme survival. Many are rusting and old, worn at the edges from the repeated and gruelling work and a constant exposure to salt water. In the harbour shop I can't resist buying something from the kitchenware section for trawler cooks, an oval steel ladle. Hannah finds *True Shark Stories* in a quayside charity shop. Past the shipyard and the RNLI lifeboat station we notice fishing nets, barnacle encrusted buoys, rusting otterboards and an old wheelhouse from a decommissioned trawler looking blindly out to sea.

Built like a giant clam shell on the edge of the harbour is the Macduff Marine Aquarium. Double doors keep in the warmth like a divers' decompression chamber. Mary, Jeff, Hannah and I step inside. All of their marine exhibits are from the Moray Firth outside the window. I do feel rather predatory peering into the touch pool full of haddock, ling, gurnard and mullet, all at arm's reach. Haddock are so beautiful – delicate purples and blue hues. The tub gurnard resemble miniature art deco submarines, their fins look strapped on. The range of colours and brightness of these North Sea fish is startling and vanishes quickly in a fishmonger's. At the centre of this circular building is a tall, wide circular tank open to the air above and full of seawater pumped directly from the sea. Hundreds of fish, including huge majestic cod, swim in and out of swaying sea kelp. Haddock are easy to spot once Mary points out St. Peter's mark above the pectoral fin, like a black thumb-print. A visit to an aquarium like Macduff's should be compulsory, rather like visiting a city farm or a real farm. I can now appreciate these beautiful fish as wildlife and not just stock to be harvested and eaten. Hannah is buying a few items from their shop when I notice a FISH PRICES sheet by the cash register. Slightly taken aback I wonder what it means, are they the latest prices for landed whitefish at Peterhead market? No, it's an adoption sheet. We decide to adopt a family haddock in the harbour tank and now receive their *Flotsam Newsletter*.

Jeff asks two workmen painting the Coastal Habitats Room where to buy local fresh fish – they recommend the Inshore Fish Supply across the aquarium car park. We easily find the long white building with a chimney extension at one end. Smoked fish galore, and fresh fish landed by a Peterhead trawler this morning. Haddock, salmon and crab, also mussels and rock turbot, the dark grey wolf-fish, known by local fishermen as catfish is said to have the whitest of white flesh. The owner, Stuart, asks if we'd like to see the smoke room. Two wooden slatted doors are set into the wall. Stuart opens one. Shining out from the tar darkness are rows of white haddock fillets like giant sharks' teeth in a gaping black mouth. Stuart unclips an internal ladder and skilfully drops it in. He descends into the smoke stack to extinguish the fire then closes the door, leaving a smouldering pile to smoke the fish overnight – an alchemical act. With an early supper in mind we ask his advice for a good local chipper. He's supplied fillets from last night's catch to a chippie on Duff Street. This seems to be the last link in a rather strange, even macabre, seafood chain – from marine aquarium, to fish merchant, to fish supper. It's rather like the Zoo recommending a good local butcher.

The drive up from the harbour is like an alpine village. We buy four haddock suppers from Chips'n'Things, carefully packed into flat blue boxes. Jeff finds the first lay-by out of town and parks us in front of a view of the sea. We tuck into the freshest fish and chips imaginable. Crisp tasty batter, delicate hot flakes of haddock and superb chips.

This coastline is like an open history book charting early fishing settlements, from Cullen, on the Moray Firth, to Fraserburgh and down past Peterhead south to Aberdeen. Some coastal towns have become synonymous with fish recipes such as Arbroath smokies, Cullen skink and Finnan haddie. As the herring fisheries boomed in the 1800s some villages were planned whilst others grew organically using natural harbours. The architecture here reflects the climate. Low, grey villages such as Cairnbulg and Inverallochy have ranked rows of squat houses gable-end facing the cold sea gales. The houses nearest the sea would have had their fishing boats drawn up between the buildings for protection during storms.

Another port we visit is Peterhead, an almost mystical destination, being the furthest point east in Scotland, so many fish facts seem to emanate from this cold, wet, windswept town, the 'Blue Toon'. It has the biggest white fish catch in Europe. Past the ice factory and the shipyard is Keithinch. This was the original fishing settlement in Peterhead. Instead of finding quaint cottages the small grid of streets is made up of towering gas tanks. These colossal steel-cable spindles, the size of a three-storey house, make us feel like Lilliputians. Unlike Keithinch the original fishing village in Fraserburgh is still there – Broadsea. This is where a century ago Christian Watt, who was an ordinary Fraserburgh fisherwife, wrote down her extraordinary life story, *The Christian Watt Papers*. It's a sad life of extreme hardship and a testament to the spirit and fortitude of Aberdonian people. Broadsea is a small unassuming village of long stone cottages, built simply. Standing in these still streets looking out to the cold North Sea is a haunting experience, in the distance a few fishing boats pass by. I think of Jean Cowie, another fisherwife here who in the 1800s lost her son, husband and father, all drowned together in a sudden North Sea storm. Similar circumstances forced Christian Watt to spend years at a time in the psychiatric wing on Aberdeen hospital, unable to deal with what the sea took from her. Walking past the many boarded-up shop fronts in Fraserburgh one is acutely aware of the difficulties that are now faced by depleted fishing communities every time a trawler is decommissioned. Not managing the fish stocks correctly has far-reaching consequences not just for wildlife and the food industry. In close-knit coastal communities every boat decommissioned affects an entire family network who give support to a boat, as well as the onshore services of net-making, boat-building, painting and fish-processing. But people here are optimistic that a living can still be made from the sea if it's well managed.

CERTIFICATE OF ADOPTION

This is to certify that
The Tilson Family
Have adopted Haddo
The Haddock

PERSONS USING
HARBOUR AREA

DO SO AT THEIR
OWN RISK

FISH SOLD HERE

HERRING IN OATS

Herring have been eaten here for centuries and oats are equally meshed into the culture, this simple dish is a classic pairing. The importance of herring is chronicled in the novel *The Silver Darlings* by Neil M Gunn which tells the history of a Scottish herring fishing village as it recovers from the Highland Clearances of the 18th century.

A SEASONAL SUMMER DISH IN THE NORTH EAST. IT'S POSSIBLE TO FOLLOW THE FRESH HERRING SEASON TO OTHER PORTS AROUND THE UK COAST THROUGHOUT MOST OF THE YEAR.

The Herring Industry Board recipe book which tried to entice the public in 1938 to eat more herring included 'A recipe from Buckingham Palace' for Harengs Frits Sauce Moutarde, a béchamel sauce flavoured with a vinegar-based mustard. It also mentions the trick of refreshing your oatmeal by lightly toasting it before use.

SERVES 4

salt and pepper	lard or vegetable oil
100g oatmeal, medium or fine	parsley
4 split fresh herring	lemon wedges

Place the oatmeal in a wide dish and season it. Dip each herring in the oatmeal pressing the oats in so that it is well covered.

Fry the herring in a little lard or vegetable oil, skin-side down first. Cook for 4 minutes or so on each side until brown, turning with care.

These herring used to be eaten with a dash of vinegar, though I suggest you serve with parsley and a squeeze of lemon. Have with a few rashers of bacon for breakfast or a creamy pile of mashed potato for lunch.

HERRING

ALSO SEE: *page 60*
COMMON NAMES: *Filling, full, haflin, mat-full, mattie, nun, seadan, scattan, sgadan, spent, Tom-belly, wine drinkers*
Young: *Shaltoo, shaldoo, shultoo*
Fry: *Sile*
Young: *Yaulin'*
Species: *Clupea harengus (Linnaeus)*
Family: *Clupeidae (Herrings, Shads, Sardines, Menhadens)*

Some other old Scottish names for herring: Dunbar weddar (salted herring), Glasgow magistrate (red herring), Jubilee herring (smoked herring), Mais (five hundred herring), Peeo (large winter herring).

Wha'll buy my caller herrin'?
They're bonnie fish and dainty fairin'.
Wha'll buy my caller herrin',
New drawn frae the Forth?

Lady Nairne
Caller Herrin'

Danger
Deep water

SOUSED HERRING

Finding small herring at the farmers market I get out some recipe books. I start with Alan Davidson, *North Atlantic Seafood*, in which I find Jimmy Fraser's soused herring recipe. *The Grampian Cookbook* suggests bay leaves, cloves and cider vinegar, even a pinch of nutmeg. Jimmy's version is more dour, but probably reflects how it was cooked in Scotland in the past.

SERVES 6

6 herring fillets, boned

2 bay leaves

4 cloves

6 peppercorns

1 large pinch nutmeg

1 small white onion, sliced

150ml cider vinegar

150ml water

HERRING
SEE: *pages* 60 & 93

MACKEREL
SEE: *page* 164

Preheat the oven to 190°C/ Gas Mark 5.

Roll the fillets tightly, tail to head. Place them in a shallow oven dish with bay leaves, cloves and peppercorns. Grate a little nutmeg on top. Arrange the onion slices on the fish. Pour in the vinegar and water, just enough to cover the fish.

Bake in the oven for 30 minutes. When cooked, leave to cool. Refrigerate.

Serve cold on toast – alongside smoked salmon on pumpernickel and smoked mackerel pate on oatcakes.

SMOKED MACKEREL PATE

SERVES 8 (1 LARGE TABLESPOON EACH)

300g smoked mackerel fillets

juice of 1 lemon

150g low-fat cream cheese

2 teaspoons horseradish

ground black pepper

Skin and de-bone the fillets thoroughly using your fingers, checking them over twice for small bones.

Add the lemon juice, cream cheese, horseradish and black pepper. Mix it using a fork until it becomes a creamy consistency, or whiz it for 30 seconds or so in a food processor if you prefer.

Refrigerate. Serve cold.

HORSEMUSSEL BREE

We find Peterhead on a tranquil Sunday and watch two fishermen sitting by their trawler-winch, mending nets. There's a splashing commotion in the water below. Hannah suddenly spots a large, whiskered face come out of the green depths munching a fish – a huge grey seal. More splashing reveals six more of these beauties, lounging in the cold water, paws folded across their chests. The fishermen who have been feeding them tell us it's a rare sight to see seals in the harbour, they'd followed the boat in. Back at the farm on a cold winter's day this soup is what you want for lunch.

SERVES 3

20 live mussels

1 stick celery, chopped

1 white onion, chopped

½ leek, chopped

2 tablespoons butter, or a little rapeseed oil

¼ teaspoon grated nutmeg

600ml dry cider

200ml water

salt and pepper

1 tablespoon butter, optional

1 tablespoon plain white flour, optional

parsley, optional

3 tablespoons single cream, optional

Wash the mussels well, scrub the shells and pull off any stringy beards or barnacles. Throw away any that are broken or don't close when tapped.

In a saucepan saute the celery, onion and leek in butter until cooked.

Add the nutmeg to the pan, stir once or twice then add the mussels, cider, water and season.

Cover the pan and bring up to a gentle simmer. Cook for a few minutes, until all the mussels have opened.

Take the mussels out with a slotted spoon. Remove the meat from all of the shells, keeping a few shells for decoration.

Sieve the liquid into a bowl. Discard the vegetables.

You now have a choice to make either a rustic soup or a smooth soup. Cream can be added at the end to either version.

Rustic version. Pour all of the liquid into the pan, bring to a boil, reduce heat. Add the cooked mussels and serve with a handful of chopped parsley.

Smooth version. Melt a tablespoon of butter, add a tablespoon of flour and whisk together to make a roux, cook a few minutes. Add 1 cup of the liquid, simmer and stir out any lumps. Slowly add the remaining liquid, bring to a boil, reduce the heat, add the cooked mussels. Use a food processor to whiz the soup until smooth. Sieve out any bits and serve with a little parsley.

NORTHERN HORSEMUSSEL

COMMON NAMES: *Horse mussel, clabach dubh, clabbie dubhs*
SHETLAND: *Yaug*
SPECIES: *Modiolus modiolus, (Linnaeus, 1758)*
FAMILY: *Mytilidae (Sea Mussels)*

Horse mussels are often called *clabbie dubhs, clab-dubh* meaning large, black mouth in Gaelic.

According to the journal *Science* the beards of mussels, called byssal threads, are partially made of iron, which is why they can anchor themselves so efficiently to rocks and ships. Scientists are hoping to create a synthetic version, a substance that has a soft, stretchy centre and a hard extensible exterior. Theoretical applications could include use in ropes, body armour or even body implants.

PARTEN BREE

BROWN CRAB
COMMON NAMES: *Edible crab, brown crab*
SPECIES: *Cancer pagurus, Linnaeus, 1758*
FAMILY: *Cancridae (Rock Crabs)*

A thick, creamy, ivory-coloured crab soup. Partan bree is a north-eastern Scottish speciality. Partan is Gaelic for crab and bree is a Doric term for soup/brew. Doric is the language spoken in Aberdeenshire. This soup also uses another of the world's fish sauces: anchovy essence. If you need to feed more people thin the soup with extra fish stock.

SERVES 5–8 AS A STARTER

*1kg large cooked crab, or 300g
 crab meat*

80g long grain rice, washed

600ml milk

600ml fish stock or 700ml water

salt and white pepper

*½ teaspoon anchovy essence,
 optional*

200ml single cream, optional

fresh chives or parsley

If you have a whole cooked crab, twist off the legs and claws, break open with pliers and a hammer and pick out all of the flesh. Put the shell pieces aside. Keep the white meat in a bowl. The body shell is easier to get into, lay it on its back and pry open the underbody. Remove and discard the soft grey gills, stomach sac and hard membranes. Use a spoon to take out the brown meat. Take all the shell pieces and smash up with a hammer. Put the pieces into a pan and cover with 700ml water, boil for 30 minutes, covered.

Put the rice in a pan, add the milk and crabshell stock or fish stock, bring to a simmer and cook until soft, 15–20 minutes.

Combine the rice, milk, brown crab meat and half of the white crab meat in a liquidizer and process until nice and smooth.

Return it all to the pan, season and add the anchovy essence. If you are making a thinner soup now is the time to add some more fish stock, or a light chicken stock. Bring to a boil. Add the remaining white crab meat and heat through.

Reduce the heat and pour in the cream gradually, stirring all the time, do not allow to boil. Add a little extra milk if the consistency is too thick. Garnish with chives or parsley.

HAM'N' HADDIE

Scotland is renowned for sumptuous cooked breakfasts and premium-quality smoked fish. This dish uses a Finnan haddock, which is a medium-sized fish which has been split open with the backbone to the right. They're cold-smoked over oak and should be a pale-straw colour, not dyed yellow. We always travel south with frozen fish and game in our luggage, setting the train berth temperature to zero to keep our catch cool overnight.

SERVES 3

150g smoked haddock, cut into individual bacon rasher-sized portions
3 large rashers smoked bacon
1 teaspoon butter
3 eggs

If you have a large piece of smoked haddock you may need to remove the skin and bones before frying. This can be done by placing the haddock in a flat pan, skin-side down and barely covering it with water. Bring to a boil then simmer for 4 minutes, turning the fish once. Remove the fish gently, peel off the skin and debone.

Heat the butter in a frying pan. Cook the bacon on one side and turn over. Put the fish pieces on top of the cooked bacon, cover with a lid and cook for 5 minutes on a medium to low heat. Push to the side and fry your eggs in the same pan.

Wow what a breakfast!

HADDOCK
SEE: *page 82*

SMOKED HADDOCK
A Finnan haddie is a whole haddock that has been split, brined and then cold- smoked. The Aberdeen cut has the backbone on the right of the split, in the London cut the backbone is on the left.

There are other variations: golden cutlets are made from block fillets and are usually dyed yellow. Smoked fillets are single fillets with their skin left on. Smokies, such as Arbroath smokies, are small haddocks tied in pairs, hot-smoked – they don't need further cooking.

Finnan haddie take their name from Findon, a village south of Aberdeen. It's a coastline dotted with fish recipe-associated placenames.

FITTIE

It's the day before New Year's Eve and we're on Aberdeen Beach between the two great rivers, the Don and the Dee. Storms of 70mph are forecast for Hogmanay. Along the beach the low winter sun provides just enough warmth for Hannah, Jeff and me to explore the shoreline, but our feet don't leave the esplanade. Instead of hunting for shells on the frozen sand we walk to the mouth of the Dee. Small roofs in the distance protrude over the esplanade, a strange sight so close to the beach. Rising from the frozen beach to their eaves is a long, concave-scalloped concrete wall. Above is a continuous pitched roof of roughly hewn slate which stares blankly at the sea. This row of twenty ancient stone cottages sit with their backs to the waves, facing the land. Their views don't linger on the sea, although you can hear and smell it. A narrow, sand-covered alleyway separates the concrete wave breaker from the houses. The whole structure must suffer extraordinary wind erosion from the constant North Sea battering. This is the fishing village of Footdee, locally called Fittie. About 85 small houses and cottages huddled together in a grid of pedestrian streets around four small squares. A church sits on the communal green. Like the Venetian fishing island of Burano, the doors here were once painted in individual colours to help identify them for returning fishermen. The stone cottages are interspersed with small huts, block built, some with harling, some wooden as if reconstructed from old ships risen out of the ground. Many are decorated with nautical themes, some with Christmas decorations. Footdee has always been separated from Aberdeen, in the past by ship building and fish processing. Today a view of the city is blocked by gas towers, transit sheds, cranes, storage cylinders, warehousing, empty lots and the quayside.

On the beach in front of Fittie are a million small mussel shells, I think of the fisher-wives and children who used to bait 'sma lines' with mussels. I see larger *yoags* (horse mussels) and *spoots* (razor clams). I pick a shell out for Jeff. Back in the car I read in the *Press & Journal*, 'Scientists says Footdee beach radiation could be a threat to young children.' The radiation is thought to have been pumped out by a nearby pipeline from a de-scaling plant run for the oil and gas industry. Existing businesses blame a fertilizer factory in the 60s and 70s. Maybe the minute shell I found should be checked with a geiger counter.

The rolling farmland, sand dunes and craggy coastline of Aberdeenshire are built from a rich colour palette which shifts with each season, enhanced in turn by glistening frost, luminous fog or crystal clear sunshine. As I sit on the fishing boat looking up at the puffins' flight paths, I imagine the sea below with mackerel and cod among the kelp beds and become aware of the joined-up nature of this landscape. It doesn't stop at the shore-line – it's a continuous eco-system. The cliffs and hills slide into the sea, extending a sense of local atmosphere under the waves in the colours, textures and patterns of its geology and wildlife. It's hard to known where Aberdeenshire stops, perhaps it's somewhere out in the North Sea.

It's been a revelation to closely observe North Sea fish both in an aquarium and flapping at the end of a fishing line. I'm more aware of their natural history and of their beauty. While I still don't feel an empathy with the fish that we routinely eat, I do appreciate the importance of their place in our shared eco-system.

WE HAVE SEEN THE FRINGES OF THE
COMMERCIAL FISHING INDUSTRY. TRAWLERS,
AUSTERE HARBOURS, FRAGMENTS OF NET
WASHED ASHORE ON FROZEN BEACHES
AND THE ECHOES OF OLDER FISHING
COMMUNITIES. I'M FINDING THAT A FISH
QUEST INVOLVES MORE THAN JUST RE-
SETTING MY CULINARY COMFORT-ZONE FOR
FISH BONES. GLIMPSES OF COMMERCIAL
FISHING AND ENVIRONMENTAL DISASTER
SEEM TO SWIM AROUND EVERY PLATEFUL. MY
CULINARY SEAFOOD PATH HAS SO FAR TAKEN
THE FAMILY FROM A LAGOON TO TWO SIDES
OF THE NORTH SEA SHARING A NAUTICAL
HISTORY – NOW I WANT TO SEE AN OCEAN.

NEW YORK CITY

BLACK FISH
BLUE FISH
ME FISH
YOU FISH

MY GROWING PASSION FOR FISH HAS SO FAR BEEN CONFINED TO LAGOON AND SEA. A BUSINESS TRIP IS TAKING US TO NEW YORK. WHERE DO OUR NEW YORKER FRIENDS SOURCE THEIR SEAFOOD? IS THERE A SENSE OF THE NEARBY ATLANTIC OCEAN? I NEED TO LEARN TO LOOK FOR WHAT'S LOCAL.

Bluefish
10-15cm small — "snapper blues"
↑ "snapper"
oh fried ↓

"harbor blues"
next size up
↓ referred huffer grilled
to small
ones - still fierce frighty fish.

sam
"cocktail
blues"

Bluefish — treat w mackerel

Weakfish, squteague
cynosiun regalis

local cider?
onion platters
GIN

chickick.
grey seatrout
grey weakfish
sand trout
seatrout
squit
weakie
weakmouth trout

SHOPPING LIST. DAY
GROLSCH — replacement
plain "00" flour
Beer for batter
LEMONS
Whitewine 2785
PAPRIKA
PARMESAN
RICE — basmati
LIMES — + flrs + herb fr
ceviche

CHILLI
PARSLEY
VEG

HOT DOGS COLD BEACH

Twenty years ago a snowstorm drove hard against the eastern seaboard of North America all week. Outside the sixth-floor apartment window Alphabet City was transformed into a smooth white undulating mass. As a thirtieth birthday treat my friend Adam and I were to spend the day touring the city in a borrowed car, a rare event. Few of my New York friends had cars in 1988. Those that did owned weather-beaten wrecks for fear of theft. These steel hulks looked like TV-cop-show props – wide, blocky, brown and tan with lots of intricate trim and peeling paintwork. After prowling about Lower Manhattan we found ourselves out at the far edge of Brooklyn on Coney Island.

Surprisingly this was my first shoreline view of an ocean. It was not however a romantic windswept, craggy sweep of coastline whose foggy silhouette was punctuated by elegant conifers. Instead I was standing on the three-mile wooden boardwalk holding a Nathan's Famous hot dog in one hand and in the other a waxed tub of cheese fries, cheese dripping gently onto the slatted wood decking. The glorious hot dog was invented here in 1867 by Charles Feltman. Nathan's opened its store in 1916. We ate ours facing the Atlantic.

The faded seafront amusement park attractions such as the parachute jump and Thunderbolt roller coaster turned their dilapidated metal backs on the ocean, like rusting dinosaur skeletons. The boardwalk held back nature so we could gaze out at the crashing waves of the Atlantic without getting our city shoes covered in sand. The severe windchill made facing the ocean almost unbearable but, not being able to resist we ventured out onto the cold empty sand towards the shoreline. Grey ice clung onto dark rocks at the water's edge. There was no sense of fish or fishing here as I scanned the horizon. The ocean did feel different to the seas I'd known – if only because of its vast imagined scale. On the grimy sand I found an airline safety card in Arabic washed ashore, a tragic item to see and a reminder of how much I take crossing the Atlantic for granted. I picked it up to add to the day's flotsam.

Twenty years later I'm in a more familiar relationship with the Atlantic Ocean, 37,000 feet above it in a 747, sitting next to Jeff and Hannah. As the plane makes a sweeping arc towards the eastern seaboard the Grand Banks are below. Their depths hold the bones of generations of fishermen and women, a roll call from ports such as Gloucester, Saint John and Halifax. It's also a graveyard for cod, a permanent reminder of how overfishing and inaccurate science wiped out the fish stocks here. Fishing was suspended in 1992 and is now extended indefinitely.

My in-flight reading has shifted over the years to reflect what I'll be up to when I disembark at JFK. Today my mind is slowly becoming lost in *North Atlantic Seafood* by Alan Davidson. It will be a pleasure using his book on the west side of the Atlantic, it was one of the first cookbooks to deal with an entire ocean, encompassing all its myriad shores. Most confine themselves to a single coastline, often delineated by an arbitrary, non-geophysical national border such as that between Spain and Portugal, missing the opportunity to describe how different nations and fishermen deal with similar catches. The recipe section in Davidson is organised by nation as each country harvests different species from the same waters. Some species are avoided because of an association with poverty, such as mussels in Scotland, which were used as bait, not food. My copy is heavily annotated with margin notes: where I bought a specimen, what it cost and how I cooked it. Recent additions strike out several fish species or entire categories, such as large predators, as being too rare to eat. Because Davidson's book contains most of the edible fish in the Atlantic there are many recipes and species of fish that wouldn't have been landed at fish markets when

the book was published in 1979. Now they're being rediscovered in the kitchen. So happily I can add notes on rod-caught bass, certified trap-caught lobsters, farmed clams and all manner of fish whose fisheries have been approved as being relatively sustainable. To help me decide what local fish to look for I've asked a few friends, visited blogs such as Ed Levine's *Serious Eats: New York*, and Nina Lalli's *Eat For Victory*, and read old *New York Times* articles. I have a list. With fish names like blackfish and bluefish I know I need to be careful as it takes a while to get a definitive description. Black sea bass are also called blackfish. Blackfish don't seem to be named in the guides, they're sometimes called tautog. Weakfish (sea trout) and fluke (summer flounder) look promising too, although fluke are out of season. Then there are the clams: cherrystone clams, littleneck clams and cockles to name but a few. Hannah's in-flight viewing is even nautical – *SpongeBob SquarePants*.

The plane finally makes its descent into JFK. The metal gantry linking the aircraft to the terminal building feels deceptively warm, but once out in the queue for cabs we're glad we have heavy coats. A freezing wind is whipping over the Atlantic shoreline. The route from JFK into Manhattan is strewn with familiar landmarks: the Lincoln Inn Motel looking like something out of an offbeat Jim Jarmusch movie, a favourite water tower, a familiar green-painted steel overpass, wooden clapperboard houses similar to the one the artist Joseph Cornell lived in, and graffiti and trash. The multi-laned freeway rises and slices through poorer neighbourhoods. Many blocks are rundown, buildings propped up with steel advertising hoardings that look in better repair than the houses below. Some of these freeway-edged houses poke their top floors above the parapet of the concrete crash barrier, looking like ornately carved tombstones facing the traffic only a few feet away. The cab passes by the Shea Stadium whose large neon baseball players look like tamed Bruce Nauman sculptures. Sonic Youth are on the radio. The constant LED traffic-diversion signs read like Jenny Holzer installations. A synchronous moment. It's hard for me to untangle the New York landscape from its 20th-century art, the cityscape exudes it. Crossing the Queensboro Bridge frames the oncoming Manhattan skyline perfectly. Late wintry evening light flattens the view, a gun-metal blue sky with a burnt umber silhouette of buildings below, splattered with windows the colour of twinkling lemon sorbet. Christmas lighting illuminates the graceful Empire State Building.

As my fear of fish subsides, replaced instead by an insatiable curiosity, I begin to realise what I've been missing all these years. One of the joys of cooking is the sense of connection it brings to generations of cooks. Family or friends might telephone to find out what the other is cooking, or to ask a question about deep-frying pheasant or what to do with venison. When faced with a fish to cook I'm beginning to feel a more fundamental connection, back to our hunter-gatherer past. Fishing itself is such a primal act. As I found in Scotland, its influences are deeply embedded along our coastlines, shaping communities over centuries. These associations permeate the kitchen when you have a fish to cook.

From a purist's point of view wild seafood is hard to beat as an indisputable local ingredient. Imported crops, domesticated fowl and farm animals have camouflaged any hope of creating a purely indigenous meal almost anywhere on the planet. This makes fresh wild fish a perfect starting point for anyone interested in indigenous ingredients.

Retracing our favourite culinary haunts with my growing love of fish I find them full of surprises. In Aberdeenshire and Sweden I had been aware of a lurking seafaring past. In New York there were always too many other distractions – I've never looked beyond the city. It's a coastline with a long seafaring past dotted with fishing ports. The largest of these is Montauk, featured in the novel *Jaws* by Peter Benchley, and whose fishing roots are traced back to the Native American Algonkians in the memorable book *Men's Lives* by Peter Matthiessen. I wonder if the presence of this local fishing industry and its history penetrates into the avenues of New York City, a metropolis of 8 million.

I'm woken by a steam-fed radiator talking to another radiator in the next room, they click, bang and wheeze at each other on an hourly basis. We're staying downtown with friends Peter, Linda and their son Ronnie. Outside snow is swirling in updraughts against the apartment block. I pull out another fish book from my luggage. Church Street rattles and shudders from the constant stream of trucks to-ing and fro-ing from Ground Zero a few blocks south. The wide snow-covered road is stained with streaks of ochre-coloured earth from the site.

I get out my list of locally caught fish and wonder which can be eaten with a clear conscience and where to find them. I've spent month after month online, reading industry reports and scientific papers, surrounded by piles of books and safe-seafood guides from around the world. For New York I've brought two. The first is a *Monterey Bay Aquarium North East Seafood Guide* which is stapled into my travel diary, this is aimed at domestic shoppers. I also have the *Seafood Choice Alliance Sourcing Seafood Book*, aimed at chefs and culinary professionals.

If you live near a small fishing community you'll probably have information of your own to make an educated choice about what to buy, but the majority of us urban dwellers need help. Some are available as internet widgets or apps meaning you can upload an interactive guide to your phone. You no longer have to watch the daily news to be up to date with overfishing before shopping. They're also useful when confronted with a restaurant menu as many don't divulge their sourcing, camouflaging their fish selection with the smokescreen of 'fresh fish selected at the market'. Perhaps restaurateurs are too close to the public's conservative and limited expectations of seafood – tuna, salmon, prawns. Some recent seafood cookbooks include passion filled ecological mission statements only to be followed by recipes for bluefin tuna and smoked eel.

BAKED BLUE

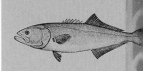

Using an online *Field & Stream* fish finder for game fish I find bluefish. In Venice they are rather confusingly called *pesca bianca*. Jane Grigson's *Fish* book refers to a recipe in *The Long Island Cook Book*. But I want to cook a recipe from Alan Davidson's *North Atlantic Seafood* whilst in New York. This is a variation of a dish he discovered in Connecticut. Other versions I've found of this recipe add rosemary, tarragon and mushrooms to the dish. Bluefish, like mackerel, can handle such additional strong flavours easily. Parmesan is also sometimes used as part of a breadcrumb/cheese crust for baking or frying fish. Here it adds richness and saltiness.

SERVES 6

1 large knob unsalted butter
1 teaspoon chopped fresh thyme
4 bluefish fillets
4 tablespoons chopped flat-leaf parsley
1 glass dry white wine
20g grated parmesan

Preheat the oven to 220°C / Gas Mark 7.

Add the butter to a shallow ovenproof dish large enough to place the fillets in one layer. Put in the oven for 10 minutes, until the butter begins to brown.

Add half the thyme and the bluefish fillets skin side up in one layer. Sprinkle the remaining thyme and parsley on top. Bake in the oven for 5 minutes.

Remove briefly to pour over the white wine and sprinkle with parmesan, return to the oven for a further 5 minutes or more depending on the thickness of the fillets. If you have a grill, give the fish a quick, hot blast for a minute to crisp the crust.

Take each fillet out carefully. Serve with the cooking juices.

BLUEFISH

COMMON NAMES: *Bluefish, sea wolf, chopper, elf, fatback, Hatteras blue, horse mackerel, rock salmon, skipjack, slammer, taylor*
Small: *Snappers, snapper blues*
Medium: *Harbour blues, cocktail blues*
SPECIES: *Pomatomus saltatrix (Linnaeus, 1766)*
FAMILY: *Pomatomidae (Bluefishes)*

Bluefish are ruthless, fierce fighting fish, making them a popular sports fish – in fact 65% of the total allowable catch is allocated to anglers. Known as the 'gangsters of the sea', bluefish move in large ravenous schools – like open-sea piranhas.

Bluefish need to be eaten fresh as they spoil quickly, and can also be bought smoked.

TILAPIA WITH GINGER & ORANGE SAUCE

Peter makes a reduced orange and ginger sauce – it takes 2 hours! Wonderful. I make some plain rice to go with it and leek and carrots which we overcook twice! We save them with some grated parmesan. A Scandinavian guest tells us that dill in Finland is much stronger-tasting because it's grown so far north. You can also catch pike in the ocean there because the salinity of the sea is so low. Fishermen there often catch freshwater river-fish in their nets far out at sea. This sauce would work well with most white fish.

SERVES 2

1 small onion, finely chopped
3 cloves of garlic, crushed
1 tablespoon olive oil
juice of 5 oranges
juice of 1 lemon

3cm cube fresh ginger, peeled
1 teaspoon grated fresh ginger
sunflower oil
4 tilapia fillets

In a heavy-based pan saute the onion and garlic in a little olive oil until translucent. Add the orange juice, lemon juice and cube of ginger. Simmer on the lowest possible heat for about 1 hour to reduce it by about a third.

Before serving grate the remaining fresh ginger into the sauce, heat through.

In a large non-stick frying pan, cook the tilapia fillets in a little sunflower oil on a medium heat for about 2 minutes on each side.

Serve with the orange and ginger sauce.

TILAPIA

COMMON NAMES: *Blue tilapia, Mozambique tilapia, Nile tilapia, St Peter's fish, izumidai, cherry snapper, lemon snapper, blue tilapia, kurper bream, largemouth kurper, Java tilapia, wami tilapia*

SPECIES: *Oreochromis; including: O. niloticus (Linnaeus, 1758), O. mossambicus (Peters, 1852), O. aureus (Steindachner, 1864), and O. urolepis hornorum (Trewavas, 1966)*

FAMILY: *Cichlidae*

Tilapia are herbivorous and can be farmed without much fishmeal. Unlike tuna or salmon they produce more protein than it takes to farm them.

There are plans to develop organic farms for tilapia. They can be farmed in closed inland systems which avoids the fish escaping and threatening marine habitats and native fish populations.

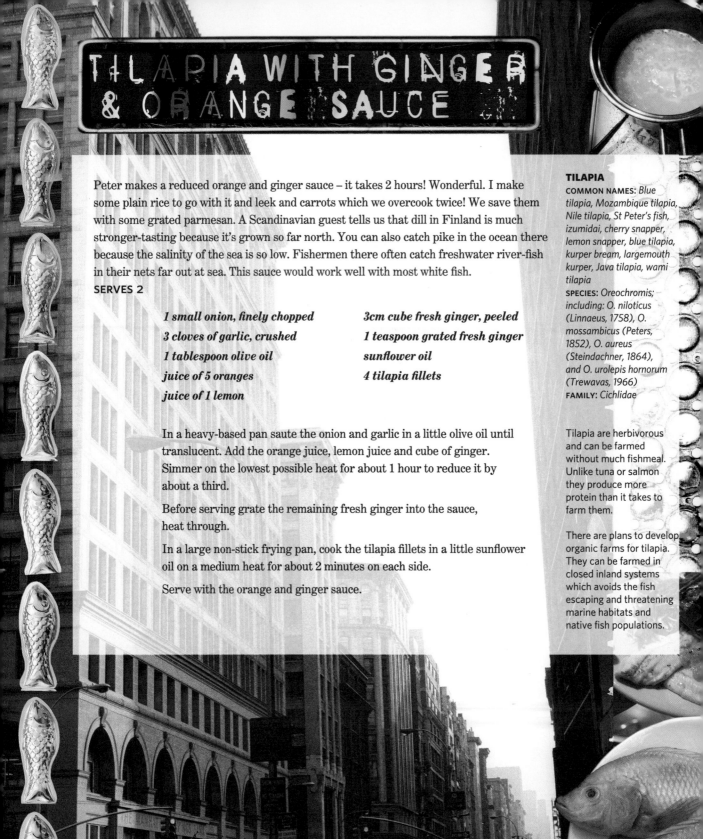

SALMON & DILL BAKED FISH CAKES

PINK SALMON
COMMON NAMES: *Pink salmon, humpback salmon*
SPECIES: *Oncorhynchus gorbuscha*
(Walbaum, 1792)
FAMILY: *Salmonidae (Salmon)*

I've been frying fish cakes for a while now, but having them cook in the oven makes them a much easier dish to serve to guests. Thank you Hannah Rapport for the idea of serving them on spinach and beetroot pickle.

SERVES 4

2 x 200g cans of wild red Alaskan salmon

3 small potatoes, boiled and roughly mashed

2 tablespoons mayonnaise

1 tablespoon grain mustard

1 handful finely chopped dill

2 tablespoons chopped chives

3 spring onions, finely chopped

black pepper

Mix all the ingredients together in a bowl and mash with a fork. Refrigerate for an hour or so.

Preheat the oven 200°C/ Gas Mark 6 and oil an oven tray.

Form the mixture into egg-like shapes with the aid of two spoons dipped in water. This is done by taking up a spoonful of fish mix with one spoon, then scooping this mix out with the other spoon – this makes a rough egg-like shape. I often have to do it a few times. Place these cakes gently onto the tray. Be careful not to knock the tray at this stage as the fish cakes are delicate.

Drizzle the fish cakes with a little olive oil, and bake for 30 minutes.

Serve with beetroot pickle (see below) and cooked spinach.

BEETROOT PICKLE

SERVES 4, WITH LEFTOVERS

1 onion, finely chopped

olive oil

5 medium beetroot, peeled and grated

3 teaspoons ground cumin

½ teaspoon ground nutmeg

4 tablespoons balsamic vinegar

In a wide frying pan saute the onion in a little olive oil until translucent.

Add the beetroot, cumin, nutmeg and a little more olive oil. Stir-fry for a few minutes, then add the balsamic vinegar. Cook gently a few minutes, stirring. Partially cover with a lid and continue to cook for 20 minutes, stirring occasionally.

Leave to cool completely. Serve cold.

CRAB CAKES

JONAH CRAB

COMMON NAMES: *Jonah crab, rock crab, Atlantic Dungeness crab, white crab*
SPECIES: *Cancer borealis Stimpson, 1859*
FAMILY: *Cancridae (Rock Crabs)*

Found on the Atlantic coast of North America.

STONE CRAB

COMMON NAMES: *Florida stone crab, Gulf stone crab, stone crab*
SPECIES: *Menippe adina, and Menippe mercenaria (Say, 1818)*
FAMILY: *Xanthidae (Mud Crabs)*

A prolific crab – they can spawn up to 13 times a year. Usually sold cooked. Found in the western North Atlantic, from North Carolina to Belize, including Texas, the Gulf of Mexico, Cuba and the Bahamas.

Peter's divine recipe is his own, developed from enjoying crab cakes in some restaurants and hating them in others, wondering what the restaurants got wrong. From watching Peter cook them I notice the frying part is tricky. On this occasion the Jonah crabs win outright – holding together better and tasting more crabby than Stone crab.

IN THE SPIRIT OF SOURCING LOCAL MARINE LIFE PETER AGREES WE SHOULD TRY OUT TWO CRAB SPECIES IN OUR CRAB CAKES.

SERVES 4

1 white onion, finely chopped
1 small fennel bulb, coarsely grated
1 carrot, grated
1 bunch tarragon, stalks discarded, finely chopped
3 tablespoons grain mustard
4 tablespoons low-fat mayonnaise

4 tablespoons breadcrumbs, plus extra for coating
1 teaspoon hot smoked paprika (optional)
juice of 1 lemon
680g lump crab meat
olive oil

In a bowl combine all of the ingredients except the crab meat and olive oil, mix well. Now gently stir in the crab meat, the mixture needs to be firm but not dry, add more mayonnaise if needed. Cover and refrigerate for at least 45 minutes.

Remove from the fridge. Heat a thin layer of olive oil in a wide frying pan. Using your hands, form the crab mix into cakes about 8 centimetres wide and 3 centimetres thick. Flip them from palm to palm to shape them. Roll the cakes in breadcrumbs and gently place in the hot oil. Don't overcrowd the pan, it's better to cook two batches.

Fry gently over a low to medium heat – cook them slowly. Add extra oil if the pan gets too dry. Once you can see a golden brown tinge around the edge the first side is cooked. This may take 8 to 10 minutes.

You only get one chance to flip them over as they're delicate. Slide a spatula under the crab cake. Keep the crab cake steady with your other hand by holding it on the top, turn it over gently. If it really falls to pieces add some more breadcrumbs to the remaining mixture before making more patties. Cook for a further 8 to 10 minutes, until browned.

Peter serves them alongside a side salad of lettuce, grated apple and a mayonnaise dip.

Variations

Some crab cakes I've found include adding: Worcestershire sauce, Tabasco, lemon juice, dry mustard or horseradish. Sometimes an egg is added to help bind the cakes together, although the mayonnaise should be enough.

CHINESE STEAMED SEA BREAM

Wandering around Chinatown reminds me of this simple and delicious way to cook fish. I particularly love the final touch of cooking the spring onions by just drizzling hot oil over them. If your steamer dish has enough depth to it you could add a layer of pak choi or fresh spinach as you steam the fish.

SERVES 3

6 mushrooms, thinly sliced

1 small piece of ginger, cut into thin slices

6 spring onions, cut into long thin slices

2 whole gilthead sea bream, gutted and cleaned

1 tablespoon light soy sauce

2 unsmoked bacon rashers, cut into thin slices

2 tablespoons peanut or vegetable oil

Find a shallow dish that will fit in a steamer. On the dish make a bed of half of the mushrooms, ginger and spring onions, and place the fish on top. Cover with the remaining ginger and mushrooms, soy sauce and bacon.

Place the steamer over a pan of boiling water, cover with a lid and cook for 20 minutes, or until the fish is cooked through.

Heat the peanut oil in a pan.

Place the remaining spring onion slices on top of the fish. When the oil is piping hot, drizzle it over the spring onions.

GILTHEAD SEA BREAM

COMMON NAMES: *Sea bream, gilthead, silver sea bream*
SPECIES: *Sparus aurata (Linnaeus, 1758)*
FAMILY: *Sparidae (Porgies)*

Like tilapia, gilthead sea bream can be farmed in inshore closed systems. As such their impact on other marine life can be minimised through good farming techinques.

BASS & HORSERADISH & SOUR CREAM SAUCE

Striped bass are a popular sports fish on the East Coast and are also farmed and caught wild commercially. The rather battered *Fishing Guide* I find in a flea market calls them spirited, and says they are often caught standing on a beach casting into the surf. Today I've bought a large one to fillet. The leftover sauce is tasty cold.
SERVES 3

20g butter	salt and pepper
4 tomatoes, chopped	3–4 striped bass fillets, or bass, skinned
2 tablespoons sour cream	10 basil leaves
2 tablespoons horseradish	olive oil

To make the sauce melt the butter in a pan and add the tomatoes. Cover and simmer over a moderate heat until the tomatoes are cooked. Now either blitz the tomatoes briefly in a blender, then return to the pan, or take the pan off the heat and use a hand-blender. Either way make sure the tomato skins have been pulverized.

Stir in the sour cream, horseradish and seasoning and bring back to a simmer. Remove from the heat and keep warm.

Preheat the grill.

If the fillets are long, cut them in half to make them easier to flip during grilling. Make a few small incisions across each fillet and push a whole basil leaf into each slit. Brush with a little olive oil.

Grill the fillets under a moderate heat for about 3 minutes each side.

Pour a little sauce onto each plate, place the fillets on top and cover with more sauce. Serve with wholegrain couscous and steamed courgettes.

Variations
Use tarragon instead of basil.
Toss the fillets in 150g of yellow or white corn meal with some seasoning, shake in a bag, remove excess cornmeal then pan fry until crisp.

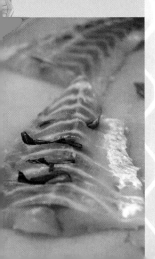

BLACK&BLUE

I'm beginning to develop some intuition when looking for and handling fresh fish but knowing whether they're cooked or not is another knack I need to perfect. I'm told that a fish is cooked when the heat penetrates to the bone – that's it, done. The flesh will then come away from the bone and be opaque rather than translucent. It can be tested by using a skewer or a narrow knife to poke a small hole to reveal the backbone of the fish to check that the flesh has cooked through. Cooking fresh prawns in Venice revealed the process in front of my eyes as the prawns turned pink. Recipes that do the same for fish are citrus, or vinegar-marinated dishes such as ceviche, escabeche and even soused herring. There are variations in most coastal cultures. Observing small cubes of sea bream marinating in lemon juice, the translucent fish slowly clouds and becomes opaque in a matter of minutes – in effect I'm watching the cooking action of the lemon juice. I once saw a plate of fish carpaccio served by mistake on a plate that was too hot, it turned the fish opaque in 10 seconds.

SERVES 4

juice of 1 lime
salt and pepper
2 blackfish fillets, cut into small cubes
2 bluefish fillets, cut into small cubes
1 handful finely chopped coriander
1 tomato, finely chopped

30 minutes before you intend to eat this, combine the lime juice, salt, pepper and fish pieces in a bowl. Turn the fish with your fingers to coat them well. Cover and refrigerate for 20 minutes. The aim is to catch the flesh just as it turns from being translucent to slightly opaque.

In another bowl add the coriander and tomato, then add the marinated fish and a little of its marinade.

BLACKFISH
COMMON NAMES: *Blackfish, tautog, white chin, chinner, tog, black porgy*
SPECIES: *Tautoga onitis (Linnaeus, 1758)*
FAMILY: *Labridae (Wrasses)*

This dark wrasse can be confused with Black sea bass (*Centropristis striatas*), which is also called blackfish. The blackfish is called a chub or oyster fish in North Carolina.

YOUR
NUMBER
35
WHEN CALLED
IT'S YOUR TURN
FOR SERVICE
GLOBE TICKET CO.
PRINTED IN U.S.A.

BAKED STRIPER CAPONATA

STRIPED BASS
SEE: *page* 121

The sweet and sour of caponata works beautifully with bass. It can be either served alongside grilled bass or baked with it in foil, as here. Being Downtown makes me think of Sicily, where caponata originated. Perhaps I've watched *The Godfather* too often. Caponata is also good baked with whole red mullet or gurnards.

SERVES 4

500g aubergines, cut into small cubes

olive oil

2 celery sticks, chopped

1 white onion, chopped

400g chopped tomatoes

100g pitted green olives, sliced lengthways

30ml red wine vinegar

3 tablespoons chopped capers

1 teaspoon sugar

2 fillets of striped bass, or bass, cut into 4 portions

1 handful chopped flat-leaf parsley

1 tablespoon lemon juice

To make the caponata, in a saucepan saute the aubergine cubes in a little oil on a moderate heat for 20–30 minutes, stirring from time to time. They need to be fully cooked. Turn out the aubergine into a cold dish and leave to cool, draining on paper towel if it seems to be too oily.

Add a little more oil to the pan and saute the celery and onion for 5 minutes. Add the tomatoes, salt, pepper and olives, cook a further 15 minutes.

Add the red wine vinegar and sugar, cook 10 minutes more. Finally add the aubergines and capers, stir and then remove from the heat. Leave to cool.

The caponata can be refrigerated, overnight if necessary. When cool, pour over the lemon juice and chopped parsley.

Preheat the oven to 220°C / Gas Mark 7.

Season the fish. On a large piece of oiled aluminium foil put two tablespoons of caponata, place the fillet on top and spoon over more caponata. Fold the foil to make a small tent, sealing the edges. Place on a baking tray and cook for 25 minutes, or until the fillet has cooked through.

FISHIN UNDER THE BRIDGE

The seafood shopping haunts of London remain a mystery to me, so New York will be a good urban training ground. Favourite shops to visit here include Eli's Vinegar Factory and Citarella, and from my sourcing research I've found The Lobster Place and Wild Edibles. I wonder which fishmongers in London a similar research process would unearth for a visiting New York foodie? Being a family trip we also need to track down a non-fish shop called Economy Candy.

I've purposely avoided visiting the New Fulton Fish Market out at Hunts Point in the South Bronx, instead I'm viewing New York fish from the street as a domestic cook. When the Fulton Fish Market moved out of Manhattan it also removed a connection to the local fishing industry. Luckily there are other offbeat opportunities to help get a sense of a city's interests – its flea markets and thrift shops. We treat them as three-dimensional reference libraries. They offer an impression of the populations' past, mapping out shifting tastes as several generations of possessions collide together to become another generation's knick-knacks. It's often more interesting to see what a city is throwing out than what it's buying new to throw out later. So before I buy some fresh fish we visit the Annex Antiques Fair & Flea Market on 25th Street and 6th Avenue. Part of the market, known as the Antiques Garage, sprawls across a multi-storey car park on West 25th Street, offering some shelter from the falling snow. Today I'm searching for a glimmer of local maritime items amongst the crowded stalls. Over the years I've built up an accumulative view of all the junk I've seen here. I recall a stall with an entire section dedicated to fishing, but it's likely the stall closed ten years ago. No stuffed fish today. I do find a small book on eastern seaboard fishing with references to bluefish and blackfish. It says that blackfish are a fine New Jersey catch, that they linger under piers and around wrecks, and are superb eating. There's a whole chapter on 'those ruthless bluefish', gangsters of the sea, telling of ravenous schools of ferocious blues, but nothing on whether they taste good. On the next stall I find a carved wooden swordfish and a frail cloth lobster pendant from Maine similar to the ones I bought in Sweden. Another stall has a sports fishing display with dozens of old rods and ancient reels, interesting to see but not necessary for me to own. Jeff finds a stunning watering can. At the market today the fish-related items reflect recreational fishing rather than the local commerical fishing fleets. The ocean feels further away. From a nearby kitchen store I buy a Maxi-Oyster shucker, a fat thermometer and 10 mini-basters.

With our local Vietnamese fish shop in London in mind I venture out onto the cold New York streets towards Chinatown to see what I imagine will be a display of non-indigenous seafood. Jeff and Hannah head uptown. Peering into the fabulous shop fronts along Mott Street, north of Canal, and into the step-down basement shops along East Broadway under the Manhattan Bridge gives me an aquatic sensory shock. Many displaced cooks try to replicate their native cuisines in their new-found kitchens. Often they'll bring along their street market culture too, and the contents of their seas and oceans. Linneaus won't help me here and neither will English. Many of the fish on display aren't seasonal and don't even attempt to look local. Over 95% must have been brought here by air. There's a sprawling Asian market look to the shops and streets with blue swimmer crabs in woven baskets, fish heads, trays of writhing eels and dried everything from oysters to squid. Buckets of huge live frogs and live fish rest in tanks, others lie gasping on polystyrene trays. Salted fish resemble piles of autumnal leaves and flattened dry octopus are like pale phantoms.

Many species I don't recognise at all, especially the shellfish and the myriad varieties of prawn and shrimp. A marine biologist would be useful as a guide. You get the feeling that if you asked for something not on view, they would cross-breed it for you in the tank-filled back-room and have it ready for you next week. Most fish are unlabeled except for price – shoppers here must know what they're looking for. Some of the displays in the step-down shops conjure images from murky deep-sea trenches. I feel like I'm getting the bends walking back up to street level.

Still needing some fish for the fridge I start my search in the large chain supermarkets. Everywhere there is an oceanic mix of wild caught fish: Domestic Atlantic, Domestic Pacific, Gulf of Mexico, Alaska, Hawaiian, New Zealand, European and probably even North Sea. Throw in farmed fish and I feel I'm sinking again. After I look up the fishmongers on my list that sell from sustainable stocks, I weave my way towards 14th Street, rummaging around checking out fresh seafood shops here and there. First is Chelsea Market. Inside a rectangular block-sized building is what appears to be a winding network of low-ceilinged tunnels cut out of rock, resembling a gold mine entrance. It's a glorious burrow full of food, stacked high with pumpkins. Food outlets selling produce and cooked food line the tunnels. Christmas decorations and delicate white lights add to the grotto experience. My destination is The Lobster Place, with its parsley edged iced displays of freshly steamed lobsters, narrow metal trays of delicate fillets – scrod, sole, hake, black cod, flounder and bluefish. And vast array of clams, oysters and scallops in wooden baskets. I buy some scrod fillets, bluefish fillets, cockles, little neck clams and a cold bag to keep my catch chilled on the way downtown. My *Sourcing Seafood Guide* lists The Lobster Place as a supplier of ocean-friendly fish, but there's no sign here today that indicates whether any fish come from a certified sustainable source or not. I imagine this will change. The quality of the fish in these selective stores looks good, firm and fresh. Most of the fish is prepared as fillets although according to a fish buyer I spoke to, shops nearer 'family' populations have a better selection of whole fish.

I find a small Wild Edibles counter nearby at Westside Market and then visit their Grand Central location. Wild Edibles provide the most information on their fish. Although they don't display scientific names they do display sustainability symbols, from relatively abundant to serious environmental impacts due to fishing methods. The labels in Wild Edibles remind me of other New York culinary shop signage at its best – informative, lengthy and sometimes funny. Although there isn't a great deal of humour to be had from describing the state of some fish these days as no sentence using the word over-exploitation can have a humorous ending. Labelling in most stores focuses on taste and cooking tips, full of enticing culinary terms: delicate flavour, fine flakes, very low-fat, meaty, firm and juicy, lettuce-like flavour, Omega 3, special-blend marinade, melt in the mouth. I have to see Citarella again. There I buy blackfish fillets, cherrystone clams, chives and thyme. Sadly my backpack is already full of fish by the time I get to Eli's Vinegar Factory on 91st Street and see their iced display of delicious-looking fish. Only tarragon remains on my shopping list. Next time I'll start here and work back downtown.

What do New Yorkers do with their fish? Wondering if there are any specialist cookbooks that might help I meet up with Jeff and Hannah and head west to one of my favourite New York culinary haunts, Bonnie Slotnick Cookbooks in Greenwich Village. While Jeff and Hannah find a boot shop nearby I explain my dilemma to Bonnie. She suggests some regional books from the Eastern seaboard fishing towns. Being a specialist used-book store means what's on offer aren't just this month's top-10 books. Instead I can look back over a century at books such as

Sensational Shellfish, The Best of The North Fork, The Taste of Gloucester, A Fisherman's Wife Cooks, Long Island Cook Book, The Complete Seafood Cookbook, Fire Island Cook Book, New England Cookbook and more. Most are books on fish and local cooking, which on Long Island means the recipes are almost 100% seafood with some game thrown in. Fish that score the most recipe entries are: bass, blackfish, bluefish, clams, codfish, crab, eel, flounder, haddock, halibut, lobster, mackerel, mussels, oysters, scallop, shrimp and weakfish. In one book alone there are an incredible 125 recipes for oyster, 70 for clams and 43 for flounder! Any community with such seasonal abundance soon grows adept at concocting recipes. In his excellent book on fish, Hugh Fearnley-Whittingstall and Nick Fisher muse that they would like to have a freshwater fish box scheme in the manner of organic veg boxes, something even better exists in Maine, the equivalent of a seawater fish box scheme. Writing in the *Washington Post* the cookery writer Nancy Harmon Jenkins talks about the Port Clyde Fresh Catch. In the summer months, like the other 200 other subscribers to Port Clyde Fresh Catch, Nancy receives 10 to 12 pounds of fresh fish a week at about $2.50–$3.00 a pound. Not only is her article a useful guide on how to deal with a weekly catch of cod, haddock and hake but it points to a growing trend of fishermen and consumers working together. The community-supported fishery based in Port Clyde, Maine, allows fishermen to market what they catch and sell it locally, such as the small pink mid-winter shrimp. As Nancy points out these local community-based fishermen are more attuned to their resources than the large commercial trawlers owned by distant fishing companies. The Port Clyde fishermen use a raised foot rope trawl to achieve a low bycatch with low-habitat impact. Conservation-orientated fishing techniques are also common to other fishing communities who are taking control of marketing and conservation of stocks. The overall aim is to catch fewer, better-quality fish that will command a higher price.

Before I reach the safety of Peter and Linda's kitchen in TriBeCa I find myself on Mulberry Street outside the Spring Lounge. Time for a drink to clear the smell of fish. The bar-counter is shaped like a question mark. I order a Smuttynose Portsmouth beer and take it to the narrow wooden bench under a plate glass window. Seen from behind the twisting neon beer-signs read like Japanese. A black pressed-tin ceiling holds a gently oscillating ceiling fan and a solitary red light bulb. This is known locally as the shark bar, a fitting place to end the day and a small reminder of what sent me on this quest. There are of course stuffed sharks, festooned this time of year with Christmas decorations wrapped in tinsel. A shark photo sits in the window under a US flag looking like a local celebrity. It's not a good place to drink more than a couple Smuttynoses if you're scared of sharks!

I get my fish back to the kitchen in TriBeCa and start unpacking, Linda tells me I have to telephone the credit card fraud squad back in London, they're suspicious of my purchases. I've obviously being buying too many clams. Between fish shopping and seeking out the unique and wonderful shop Economy Candy for Hannah I've managed to completely fill a suitcase with canned fish and sweets. It rattles. Knowing what local fish are out there in the ocean beyond the skyscrapers when confronted by a fishmonger's display felt empowering. I could side-step anything air-freighted and avoid the predictable sideshows of tuna-salmon-prawn, and king prawn-swordfish-monkfish. Instead I was able to identify, source, buy and cook fish that's local, seasonal and not on a fish-to-avoid list, all of which was extremely tasty. I'm slowly getting a real feel for fish shopping – even in the glass and steel metropolis.

EXIT

A NEW YORK MAGAZINE EDITOR HAS COMMISSIONED ME TO WRITE ABOUT A FUTURE TRIP TO AUSTRALIA WHICH WE ARE TAKING AS JEFF IS EXHIBITING THERE. THIS LANDS US ON THE VERY EDGE OF THE WORLD'S LARGEST OCEAN, THE PACIFIC.

OFF TO SEE THE WIZARD

SYDNEY & THE GREAT BARRIER REEF, AUSTRALIA

THE PACIFIC BECKONS. WITH THE LOAN OF A FISHERMAN'S COTTAGE IN SYDNEY WE HEAD SOUTH OF THE EQUATOR.

JEFF IS EXHIBITING IN SYDNEY AT THE LIVERPOOL STREET GALLERY SO WE DECIDE TO GO TO AUSTRALIA FOR A MONTH. SHE'S BOUGHT US A SPARE SUITCASE IN WHICH TO BRING BACK OUR CULINARY DISCOVERIES AND ONLINE HANNAH HAS FOUND A PIE SHOP IN SYDNEY CALLED HANNAH'S PIES. I HAVE MY EYE ON THE CULINARY SUBURBS OF SYDNEY AND THE GREAT BARRIER REEF.

WATSONS BAY

LIFEJACKET
INSIDE

SPECIAL
$13·95

SYDNEY

On the blustery autumnal streets of New York I felt a shared experience of the Atlantic Ocean. Steeped in a communal history of caravels, galleons, clippers, exploration, commercial fishing and the horrors of naval warfare, romanticised and fictionalised by childhood books and films. Its cold deep waters grasp the wrecks of the Titanic, HMS Hood, Bismarck and the many fishing boats lost at sea, such as the Andrea Gail, a swordfish boat from Gloucester.

The Pacific Ocean and Australia seems a far more exotic destination, even with constitutional ties to Britain. As a lover of maps I grew up with a Euro-centric view of the planet, shaped by a 1569 Mercator projection with the Atlantic in the centre. Only later did I have this view challenged by other world maps such as the glorious one drawn by Surrealists, who put the Pacific in the centre and Buckminster Fuller's *AirOcean World Map*, drawn on an icosahedron, which places all the world's oceans at the centre rimmed by the continents – definitely a fish-orientated view of the planet. I find our own family map of the world is constantly being questioned and re-drawn. Visiting Australia will shift the axis yet again. Until now Australia has appeared far far away and the dismal thought of twenty-six hours buckled to an economy plane seat has become less desirable with each passing year. I've produced some heavily annotated food maps of Sydney on which I've drawn walking routes and highlighted potential culinary attractions. We're ready – oven thermometer packed and a seafood field-guide ordered. Our final destination is a generous loan from friends, a fisherman's weatherboard cottage on Watson's Bay on the South Head – where the ocean meets Sydney Harbour. This narrowing peninsula is battered by waves on the Pacific Ocean side and lulled by lapping waters on the bay side, where the famous Doyles fish restaurant overlooks a distant view of central Sydney.

We arrive with no time to visit an organic farmers' market or the famed Sydney Fish Market, but we need to eat something quickly before we succumb to jet lag. The 325 bus lets us off at Double Bay near a large Woolworths, which in Australia is a food store. We cross the busy street amidst a storm that threatens to wash the supermarket into the dark waters of the bay. Hidden amongst the global foodstuffs lurks some indigenous fare such as Lamington cakes, named after Baron Lamington, Governor of Queensland in the late nineteenth century. These are small sponge rectangles dipped in chocolate and covered in desiccated coconut. We also find Vegemite, Arnott's biscuits, Keen's mustard, Cherry Ripe chocolate bars, firm blocks of cottage cheese from New South Wales, kangaroo steaks and irregular bricks of tasty haloumi. A blurry fish counter provides some faint views of what's out there in the Pacific. First night meals are often rather makeshift. We stumble back tired to our idyllic fishing cottage. I experiment with kangaroo steaks and tamarind puree, tonight's emergency back-ups for Jeff and Hannah are lamb sausages served in Turkish flat bread and haloumi fried in balsamic vinegar. Fortunately the steaks taste terrific, but we eat the sausages too.

After the possums have stopped their noisy nocturnal antics we're roused by a primordial dawn chorus as the birdlife suddenly wakens. Lorikeets, sulphur-crested cockatoos, noisy miners and silver gulls – screeching, whooping, chattering and squawking. Crimson rosellas masquerade amongst the ruby-red flowers of the stark, bare flame trees. The view from the bright wood-panelled kitchen is of mango, avocado and palm trees. It's an exotic and tropical audio-visual riot. This cottage couldn't be a more appropriate outpost to start a first-time tour of Sydney and beyond.

Watson's Bay was the site of the first landing within Sydney Harbour and like many fishing

communities, such as Footie in Abderdeen or Santa Marta in Venice, it's an isolated spot on the seaward edge of the city. Being occupied as early as 1790 it is one of the earliest European settlements and was the first fishery to help supply the colonists. Simple wooden weatherboard cottages remain, but I don't feel the presence of fishermen yet. The turquoise water in the harbour is remarkably clear, even cold rain can't diminish its beauty. With the help of melatonin we stumble onto a 1.45pm Circular Quay-bound ferry.

Sydney is a beautiful and intriguing city. The architecture, food and people are exceedingly friendly and welcoming but the underlying natural environment exudes a dark, brooding beauty at its heart that is revealed slowly, wholly alien and bewildering, setting my mind alight. I feel the entire metropolis could revert to a primeval jungle at any moment. The glorious foliage of gum trees is populated with giant undulating fruit bat colonies, an echo of deep time at work in this hidden landscape. The majestic Moreton Bay Fig trees billow like sailcloths in the cold, wet winds, their rain-streaked buttress roots erupting out of the green parkland like giant shards of sheet steel.

Sydney reminds me of Venice in the 14th century and perhaps New York in the early 20th century – a city influenced by an influx of ingredients and people. A culinary crossroads. The gastronomic map of Sydney is like viewing the Great Barrier Reef from a helicopter. Hundreds of small reefs become visible, each with their own distinct character. These neighbourhoods shift and change as new populations are washed ashore, bringing with them their own culture and food. This slow integration occurs out in the suburbs, or 'burbs as Sydneysiders call them, the seedbeds of their fusion cuisine. Our Australian friends are rather bemused and fascinated by our plan to explore the outer suburbs. I hope I'll begin to get a sense of Pacific fish. It's akin to telling our New York friends we're undertaking a historic tour of bakeries in Queens.

Arriving at Circular Quays is one of those great urban water-borne experiences. As our ferry passes by the Sydney Opera House and turns into Sydney Cove, downtown skyscrapers gradually loom up and the Museum of Contemporary Art sidles past. Like Venice, Circular Quay has water craft of every shape and size serving many destinations. You feel the urge to travel and explore. I'm desperate to visit the Sydney Fish Market so I volunteer to go shopping. A Darling Harbour ferry drops me off at Pyrmont Bay for the industrial waterfront and the Fish Market while Jeff and Hannah visit the aquarium. The market is reached through a large quayside car park circled by fishmonger outlets. Inside the market building I'm expecting to see something between the Feskekôrka, fish church, and the Fiskhamn, the commercial market in Göteborg – a melding of commercial auctions for merchants alongside stalls for domestic and restaurant use. Within sight of water that flows into the Pacific Ocean I'm also hoping to be bewildered by the fish. Sadly the business end of the market is kept at arm's-length from the casual visitor; only an early morning viewing area is provided, rather like a lecture hall. Although the surroundings may lack the mercantile charm of Mediterranean fish markets the produce on offer here is spectacular, with a hallucinatory colour palette. Most noticeable are the bi-valves and crustacea: sparkling green mussels, Sydney rock oysters being shucked as fast as they can be eaten, spanner crabs and mud crabs that look armoured in lead. It reminds me that, as I found in Scotland, local marine life reflects the onshore landscapes, as if camouflage is needed both in and out of the water. The primary activity for visitors here is eating. Hidden auction halls are flanked by a food court serving seafood prepared in any fashion you can imagine: raw, cured, smoked, steamed, fried, grilled, barbecued or baked. You can make up a picnic to eat on the dockside as there's also a baker, bottle shop (off licence), deli and grocer. I choose my lunch spot by eyeing up the hundreds of platefuls of food being eaten. The seafood at Christie's looks promising so I select a pick-and-mix plate of; sweet-chilli baby octopus, oyster Mornay, scallops, calamari and fried barramundi. Before heading for the home-bound Pyrmont ferry I buy a large locally-caught barramundi and a Balmain bug from De Costi, a market fishmonger.

One of my initial stumbling blocks on this seafood quest was confusing naming of fish. In Australia the issue is being addressed as the consistency of fish names is recognised as being a consumer issue. Being a lover of language it worries me slightly and I hope old names might appear next to Standard Names. The Australian Fish Names Standard decrees that one Standard Fish Name is to be used for each seafood species produced or traded in Australia – 4,500 seafood species in total. From 2008 all fish at the market have been named using the scheme. Back in our fisherman's cottage I unpack the unfamiliar fish – the barramundi looks fierce.

The only sharks I've seen have been plastic toys hanging outside tourist shops and a large warning sign on the beach outside the Bathers' Pavilion restaurant where I ate a pizza topped with lamb neck, pecorino, eggplant, mint and garlic nettles. Before leaving Sydney we do indeed find Hannah's Pies opposite the Powerhouse Museum in Ultimo where we eat a Curry Tiger – a spicy meat pie topped with mashed potato and a ring of mushy peas filled with gravy. It was gorgeous. Elsewhere in town we enjoy extraordinary food: at Bill's ricotta hotcakes and the best muffin I've ever tasted, and spectacular Balmain bugs at Sean's Panorama on Bondi Beach. Surrounded by Sydney's enthusiasm, culinary energy and gastronomic invention is like being invited to a non-stop food festival. It's a city you feel empowered to cook in. Walking back home along the moonlit beach on Watson's Bay the tide is in. Seagulls, lorikeets and cockatoos are asleep, misty rain covers our supermarket carrier bags, and the distant view of Sydney has changed yet again. It resembles a pile of Christmas tree lights shrouded in silver fog. Back in our fisherman's cottage the kitchen beckons, there is a family to feed then suitcases to pack as tomorrow Jeff, Hannah and I head a thousand miles north to the humid tropics of Queensland, the Great Barrier Reef and another kitchen.

GRILLED MUSSELS THREE WAYS

Two of the joys of the Sydney Fish Market are the gourmet deli and the fruit and vegetable shop. I spend a lot of time going backwards and forwards between the fish, then checking out the veg. Do they have watercress or cucumber? Back to the fish. Does the deli have feta? Back to the fish. Eventually I have everything we need. Grilled mussels are a great support for all manner of delicious toppings.

SERVES 3

10 live blue mussels
10 live green mussels
1 glass white wine

Topping 1
2 tablespoons feta, crumbled
1 teaspoon chopped pinenuts
2 tablespoons chopped mint leaves
2 tablespoons breadcrumbs

Topping 2
½ onion, finely chopped
1 fresh red chilli, finely sliced
2 tablespoons chopped coriander
2 tablespoons breadcrumbs

Topping 3
1 tablespoon chopped macadamia nuts
2 cloves garlic, finely sliced
2 tablespoons chopped coriander
2 tablespoons breadcrumbs

BLUE MUSSEL
COMMON NAMES: *Mussel, black mussel, common mussel*
SPECIES: *Mytilus edulis, (Linnaeus, 1758)*
FAMILY: *Mytilidae (Sea Mussels)*

GREEN MUSSEL
COMMON NAMES: *Green lip mussel, greenshell mussel, or kuku, or kutai*
SPECIES: *Perna canaliculus, Gmelin, 1791*
FAMILY: *Mytilidae (Sea Mussels)*

Mussels are one of the most environmentally sound seafood choices available, and they taste so good. Farmed mussels usually have thinner shells than wild-caught mussels because they are usually farmed in calm waters.

Put the mussels in a bowl of cold water. Discard any that don't close when tapped. Wash the mussels well, giving them a good scrub, remove any 'beards' that are sticking out.

Combine the topping ingredients in three seperate bowls.

Pre-cook the mussels for a few minutes in a wide pan covered with a lid, with a splash of white wine. Don't overcook them or they'll be chewy. Discard any that don't open.

Separate out the mussel shells into halves, keeping the empty shells.

The sweet tasting pan juices mustn't be wasted. Moisten some of the topping mixes with the juice.

Preheat the grill, medium heat.

Arrange the cooked mussels in their half-shells on an oven tray.

Spoon a little of one of the toppings onto each mussel.

If you have leftover toppings, fill the empty shells with them and drizzle over some of the cooking juices. Add to the tray of mussels.

Grill the mussels until the breadcrumbs are golden, about 4 minutes.

EASTPOINT
BONELESS
FLATHEAD
FILLETS
$42.99
kg

TIGER FLATHEAD

COMMON NAMES: *Deep sea flathead, flathead, king flathead, spiky flathead, toothy flathead, trawl flathead*

SPECIES: *Neoplatycephalus richardsoni, Castelnau, 1872*

FAMILY: *Platycephalidae (Flatheads)*

There are more than 40 flathead species in Australian waters.

SESAME FLATHEAD

We're so tired I can barely shop. The parking zone outside Coles at Edgecliff is only one hour. Jet lag is bad, Hannah is wobbling and then it hits me. I buy a pack of sesame seeds, and from the excellent fishmonger outside the shopping mall, some flathead fillets – they're narrow and thin and should cook quickly when we get back to the cottage. It's a bit of a cheat recipe, too easy for such a great taste. The crisp nuttiness of the sesame seeds and the moist flaky fish is wonderful. I still don't own a non-stick pan back in London. Using one here has convinced me that I should. This recipe would suit any thin fish fillet.

SERVES 3

500g flathead fillets, skinned   *1 teaspoon salt*

1 egg   *3 tablespoons sesame seeds*

120ml milk   *olive oil*

50g plain white flour

Beat the egg and milk together in a bowl.

Mix the flour, salt and sesame seeds together on a plate.

Preheat a frying pan and add a little olive oil.

Dip the flathead fillets first in the egg-milk mix then into the flour, making sure they are well covered in sesame seeds.

Add to the pan and saute on a moderate heat, turning once. The fillets are so thin they only take a few minutes to cook. Make sure the sesame seeds begin to tinge with colour.

Variation

Make a sauce/paste from 3 tablespoons each of tahini (sesame paste), olive oil, and water. Add 1 tablespoon of lemon juice. Use to marinate your fish fillets before frying or baking.

1

BLUE SWIMMER CRAB AND WATERCRESS SOUP

BLUE SWIMMER CRAB

COMMON NAMES: *Blue crab, blue manna, blue swimmer, bluey, brown mud crab, sand crab, sandy*
SPECIES: *Portunus pelagicus, (Linnaeus, 1758)*
FAMILY: *Portunidae (Swimming Crabs)*

Crab soup is one the real delights of eating seafood. What an extraordinary taste. Deep and sweet, impossible to resist. This recipe is based on one from an old battered copy of Australian *Women's Weekly* I found in a second-hand store in the Blue Mountains. Wherever crabs are caught there's sure to be a recipe for crab soup somewhere nearby. You can always spice up this soup with a little saffron or maybe even some fish at the stock-making stage.

SERVES 3

2 live blue swimmer crabs (or any medium-sized crab)
2 teaspoons butter
1 carrot, chopped
2 cloves garlic
1 white onion, chopped
1 stick celery, chopped
1.5 litres water

1 bay leaf
50ml dry white wine
50g watercress
50ml single cream
salt and pepper
Roux
30g butter
30g plain flour

The crabs can be dispatched by putting them in the freezer for 2 hours.

Remove the crab flesh from the body and claws, discarding the grey tissue.

To make your stock, melt the butter in a pan, add the crab shells, carrot, garlic, onion and celery and saute for 5 minutes. Add the water and bay leaf. Simmer, uncovered for 30 minutes. Strain the liquid and discard the remains.

Make the roux. In a pan, melt the butter and mix in the flour. Gradually add a cup of the stock, letting it thicken. Add the wine and two more cups of stock. Finally add all of the remaining stock, the watercress and the crab meat. Simmer for 5 minutes, until the crab meat is cooked.

Remove from the heat and blend the mixture in a food processor until smooth. You may need to do this in batches.

Return the soup to the pan and reheat gently without boiling. Add the cream and season to your taste.

MAX NO OF PASSENGERS ALLOWED ON THIS DECK 143

PRODUCT OF AUSTRALIA

peter's

GREEN
BLUE SWIMMER
CRABS

$11·99

kg

BARRAMUNDI IN COCONUT MILK

We've been touring the 'burbs of Sydney seeking out various ethnic cuisines. The Lebanese shops in Bankstown remind me of a recipe called *samak bi tahini,* for a whole baked fish smothered in tahini I found in an 1960s Lebanese cookbook. We've tried this sauce on whiting fillets too. They require much less sauce and extremely careful deboning as the sauce tends to hide what's underneath it. Asia has had a great influence on the cooking here. The Thai Kee Supermarket in Chinatown, from which I choose a few items to cook with barramundi, seems to have an aisle for every Asian cuisine imaginable.

SERVES 3

2 cloves garlic, finely sliced
1 inch fresh ginger, peeled, thin slices
1 white onion, finely sliced
olive oil

3 small barramundi fillets
170ml coconut milk
1 handful chopped coriander leaves

Saute the garlic, ginger and onion in olive oil until translucent.

Add the barramundi fillets and sear on each side, about a minute or so. Add the coconut milk and simmer gently for 5 minutes.

Decorate with coriander leaves and serve with rice.

Variation
Add 200g canned cannellini beans with the coconut milk.

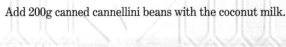

LEATHERJACKET CUCUMBER AND MINT

LEATHERJACKET
COMMON NAME:
Ocean jacket
SPECIES: *Nelusetta ayraudi,*
Quoy & Gaimard, 1824
FAMILY: *Monacanthidae*

There are more than 60 species of leatherjacket in Australian waters. Leatherjackets get their name from their skin, which needs to be removed – usually after cooking.

I'm back at the Sydney Fish Market looking for a bagful of fish for supper. I need some impartial help to choose a fishmongers to buy fish for Jeff, Hannah and Nick, a friend from London who is working here. A splendid kitchenware shop called Rosie's looks a likely source of information. I've never seen so much barbecue equipment on offer before, all for fish. I buy some small tongs. The owner recommends either Peter's in the market building or de Costi outside where I buy some beautiful leatherjackets. This recipe works well with other small fish such as sea bream.

SERVES 2

¼ cucumber, peeled and sliced
200ml fish or vegetable stock
3 tablespoons chopped fresh mint
1 leatherjacket or sea bream, be-headed and gutted
rapeseed oil

Add the cucumber and stock to a small pan and simmer gently for 10 minutes.

Remove from the heat, whiz in a food processor, return to the pan and reduce further.

Take off the heat, add the mint and keep warm.

Pan fry the leatherjacket in a little rapeseed oil for 5 minutes or so each side. Serve with the sauce.

Variation
Place the leatherjacket on a large piece of aluminium foil. Pour over the sauce and fold over the edges of the foil to make a loose package. Bake at 200°C/ Gas Mark 6 for roughly 30 minutes, or less if the fish is small, until the fish is cooked through.

Seafood

FRESH COOKED $
LOBSTER
Eastern Rock
PRODUCT OF AUSTRALIA
54·95
kg

peters PRODUCT OF AUSTRALIA
COOKED $
SPANNER 1595
CRABS

AVOCADO SEAFOOD SALAD

The key to the success of this salad is finding the best ingredients you can. If you can't find rock lobster or bugs use a mixture of lobster and perhaps some langoustine, it's the mixture of species size that's important – large medium and small crustacea are needed eg. lobster, langoustine, prawn. Avocados are a great way to make the more expensive seafood ingredients go further.

SERVES 2

1 cooked rock lobster tail

1 cooked Balmain bug

6 cooked prawns, shelled, cut into 3

½ large ripe avocado, cut into small chunks

2 tablespoons chopped macadamia nuts

1 tablespoon runny honey

1 tablespoon lemon juice

4 tablespoons olive oil

1 tablespoon white wine vinegar

1 teaspoon Dijon mustard

Carefully take all of the flesh out of the rock lobsters and Balmain bug, cut into bite-sized pieces, put into a salad bowl. Add the prawns, avocado and nuts.

Make a dressing, mix the honey, lemon juice, olive oil, white wine vinegar and mustard in a jar, shake well. Pour over the salad. Cover the bowl and refrigerate for an hour or so.

Serve with fresh bread and a chilled Australian white wine.

Variation
Also good with a little firm cooked white fish. You could extend it with some crisp chopped red peppers or a touch of lettuce, although some of the richness may be lost.

RAINFOREST REEF

1200 miles north of Sydney. During our final descent the Airshow inflight-map shows Beijing, Osaka and the Philippines. It feels as if we've reached the Far East as Kuala Lumpur, Jakarta, Manila fill the head-rest screens. We touch down in Cairns. An hour or so north, deep in the tropics, is Port Douglas, the last sizeable town before the rainforest takes over north of the River Daintree.

Port Douglas is a town founded on business, not settlement – a pioneer port hewn and chopped from the tropical rainforest to ship gold ore from the Palmer River gold field, discovered in 1873. A town held together with canvas, corrugated iron, tarpaulins and kerosene lamps. A hundred years earlier Captain Cook had sailed by this lonely coast on his ship Endeavour, and ran aground on the Great Barrier Reef; his 'ship struck and stuck fast'. It was a foreboding territory of impenetrable mosquito-ridden jungles and crocodile-filled creeks, where loaded wagons were hauled by bullocks along treacherous bush tracks, their axles deep in mud. The gold rush was followed by tin, cedar, *beche-de-mer* (sea cucumbers) and then sugar cane farms. Today diesel locomotives haul the cane from the fields to the refinery at Mossman Sugar Mill.

If I thought Sydney's environment conjured up echoes of a primordial past waiting to break through the urban fabric, Queensland is like a Jurassic volcano. A thin veneer of tarmac and concrete tries to keep the jungle at bay. The rainforest explodes and bubbles up through every vacant lot. TV tourism didn't prepare us for the breathtaking beauty of a place where two of the world's natural wonders the Great Barrier Reef and the Daintree rainforest, the oldest rainforest in the world – over one hundred and thirty-five million years – touch hands.

Our generously loaned villa has a tropical ambience with louvered shutters, ceiling fans and a view of pandanus palms. It's hermetically sealed against tropical wildlife, which is probably just as well. Stepping off the manicured fairway into a palm grove the thick compact grass gives way to crunchy, dry palm fronds, seed pods, fallen coconuts and scrubby bush. Beyond is Four Mile Beach. I'm thinking of sharks as I scan the expanse of ocean. Public warning signs declare the presence of marine stingers – box jelly fish. In case you're stung most beaches provide emergency plastic bottles of vinegar stuck into pieces of piping on poles. Enjoying the jungle backdrop we wander the beach picking up shells and looking out towards the reef. Posters pinned up outside the pool's changing room display horrendously graphic images of what the local marine life can do to your skin. Box jellyfish are the most feared, their presence a good reason to bathe in the swimming pools during the summer months, but this is winter.

As the afternoon ends squawking lorikeets dive from tree to tree in drunken squadrons, geckos materialise on walls and majestic ibis pick at trash cans – not something I'd expect from a bird I normally associate with graceful sculptures or hieroglyphics. As evening arrives so do the biggest mosquitos I've ever seen. We don't need to listen out for their high-pitched drone, we can see them coming from a distance. A whirlwind visit to an IGA supermarket beyond the town's city limit near Captain Cook Highway. Outside a humid smell emerges and lurks with the onset of night. Later as we meander along the roads and palm tree-lined multiple roundabouts of Port Douglas I roll down the window of our four-wheel drive, the thick aroma has deepened. At last I can place it – hops! Fermenting hops, or does the smell exude from the fecund jungle floor? Walking back late at night moonlit waves crash into the bases of the coconut trees leaving barely enough beach for us to walk along. We're dazzled by the vastness of the ocean and stars alike. Skink-like lizards flit about, while orange-footed scrubfowl rustle in the dry foliage, sounding larger than their size. In the darkness Hannah finds a series of steps lit by small lamps to lead us back to the golf greens and the villa.

MARINE STINGERS
ARE PRESENT IN
THESE WATERS
DURING SUMMER
MONTHS

VINEGAR

FOR USE ON MARINE STINGS
POUR ON – DO NOT RUB
SEEK MEDICAL ATTENTION

REDTHROAT EMPEROR WITH WATERCRESS & ORANGE SALAD

The exotic tropical orchards in Queensland grow a staggering variety of fruit including black sapote, durian, rambutan, breadfruit, jackfruit, mangosteen, sapodilla, soursop, sweetsop and abiu. Banana trees grow along the edge of fields full of pineapples, next door is a tea plantation. A short drive up onto the tableland and the landscape becomes a shimmering eucalyptus savannah dotted with termite mounds and kangaroos. Past the citrus groves we stop at a coffee plantation where Jeff buys a huge paw-paw straight from the tree and we taste the ripe (red) berries of the coffee bushes. The citrus fruit reminds me of the delights found in California. This recipe uses some of the locally grown oranges and would be good with any firm white fish.

SERVES 3

1 pak choi, quartered lengthways

500g redthroat emperor or sea bream fillets, skinned

1 red chilli, sliced lengthways and de-seeded

2 spring onions, chopped

5 leaves crunchy lettuce

1 bunch watercress, roughly chopped

2 oranges, peeled, de-seeded and sliced

4 tablespoons olive oil

1 tablespoon white wine vinegar

1 teaspoon Dijon mustard

Arrange the pak choi pieces on a sheet of aluminium foil. Lay the redthroat emperor fillets on top, scatter the chilli and spring onions over the fish.

Fold the foil into a loose package and place in a steamer. Cover with a lid and steam for 15 minutes.

Make a salad from the lettuce, watercress and oranges. Mix the olive oil, white wine vinegar and mustard in a jar, shake well and pour over the salad.

Remove just the fish from the steamer and place on the salad. Serve the steamed pak choi, chilli and spring onions alongside.

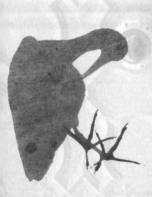

BARRAMUNDI WITH GREEN PEPPERCORNS & WILTED HERBS

BARRAMUNDI
SEE: *page* 142

There's an exotic mixture of climates in Queensland from tropical coastal to the drier tablelands, all providing an enviable diversity of fruit, vegetables, herbs, nuts and spices. Looking at the map I'm reminded we're only 300 miles from Papua New Guinea. A stall at the Farmers' Market has an amazing selection of herbs and spices in baskets and glass-lidded boxes. Fresh turmeric, clusters of green peppercorns and a basil, similar in flavour and appearance to holy basil, I've never tasted before.

SERVES 2

2 tablespoons fresh green peppercorns

2 cloves garlic, finely sliced

1 teaspoon olive oil

2 small fillets barramundi

juice of ½ lemon

3 spring onions, chopped

4 large handfuls holy basil, or a mixture of sage and basil

Fry the green peppercorns and garlic in the oil for a few minutes.

Add the barramundi fillets. Cook for 5–6 minutes each side. Add the lemon juice and spring onions and cook for 30 seconds. Add the holy basil and allow to wilt slightly.

The result should be crispy browned/burnt garlic and peppercorns, moist firm fish and fragrant, wilted herbs.

RED EMPEROR

COMMON NAMES: *Emperor red snapper, government bream, king snapper, queenfish, red kelp*
SPECIES: *Lutjanus sebae,* (Cuvier, 1816)
FAMILY: *Lutjanidae* (Snappers)

RED 'N' GREEN

It's late and we need something to eat very fast indeed. If you can pan fry the fish at the same time as making the salsa, this dish takes less than 15 minutes from fridge to plate. We ate it with bread and salad. Any firm white fish fillet would suit this green herby salsa accompaniment.

SERVES 3

600g red emperor fillets
olive oil
Green herb salsa
3 spring onions, chopped
1 handful chopped flat-leaf parsley
1 handful chopped mint leaves

1 handful chopped holy basil, or a mixture of sage and basil
2 cloves garlic, chopped
1 tablespoon lemon juice
pepper
5 tablespoons olive oil

Place all of the salsa ingredients into a blender and whiz into a rough mix – not mushy. To prevent it becoming a puree you may want to tip it out onto a chopping board and finish it off with a large knife.

Pan fry the red emperor fillets in a little olive oil for a few minutes each side.

Serve with the green salsa.

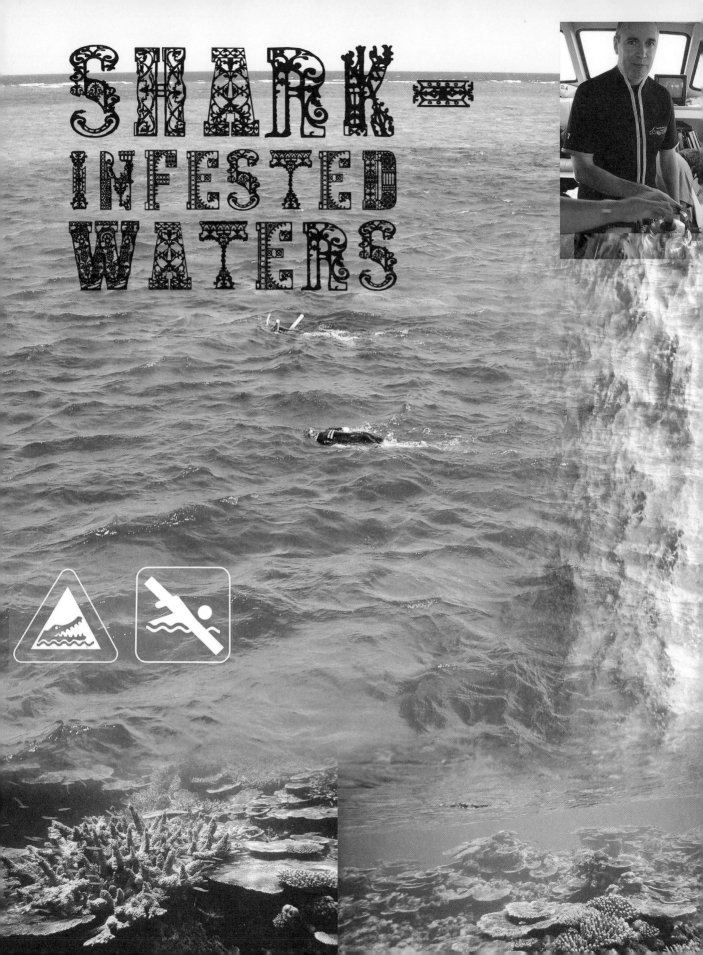

SHARK-INFESTED WATERS

Lying in bed I'm woken by glaring Pacific light. The golf course is thick with dew which lingers well into the day. You need to watch out for salties, salt water crocodiles here. They're ambush predators – not a nice thought. The poolside gossip is of an eleven-foot croc lurking on the 3rd hole and a seventeen-footer seen walking along the 10th near the Sports Bar – croc warning signs have been put up. I practise snorkelling in the safety of the pool, which I would highly recommend. I don't want a refresher course in snorkelling bobbing up and down in the depths of the Pacific tomorrow.

We've been quizzing everyone we meet about where to buy fresh locally caught fish, some recommend the fish shop in Craiglie others a shop in Port Douglas. We drive to Craiglie in the afternoon heat. Perhaps earlier might have been better as there isn't much fresh fish: some barramundi, coral trout and mahi-mahi, cooked prawn and bugs. Another shop luckily has some red throat emperor, red emperor and some good looking barramundi.

On the drive down we passed some small-scale prawn farms which take water directly from the ocean. There are basically two types of prawn: warmwater and coldwater. Warmwater prawn farms are a very 21st-century problem. When an ingredient such as warmwater prawns hits a global 'what's hot' list it shifts from being a luxury purchase to something you expect a corner sandwich shop to offer in a ciabatta roll. Demand in the mid-90s soon outweighed what could be caught wild. Mangroves were cleared across the world, ponds were dug and filled with brackish water, and farms often failed leaving behind poisoned, salinated land. We have walked through magical mangroves north of the Daintree River listening out for tree frogs, they are like coastal rainforests, delicate primeval ecosystems developed over millennia. Over 50% of the world's mangroves have disappeared, half of this is due to the cultivation of warmwater prawns. Supermarkets try to pass off these farms as being ok by using phrases such as ' farm land is generally free of mangrove population.' This is rather like saying someone is generally not pregnant. Coldwater prawns have fewer problems for the ecological cook, although they are not entirely guilt-free. So I've been avoiding the local prawns. Before going home to cook we book a day on the Great Barrier Reef at the Wavelength office. They were the first company to offer tours on the reef and have a strong belief in low-impact tourism.

In our kitchen Jeff tends our burgeoning tropical fruit collection. From the farmers' market we have bought yellow squash, ruby red grapefruit, passion fruit, mandarins, kiwi fruit, dried mango, tangelos and avocados, locally grown coffee, wattleseed and black sapote, ice cream beans and taro, grown nearby at Dimbulah. Hannah explores the more exotic items: black sapote, also called chocolate persimmon, which has a black edible flesh. She is thrilled that ice cream beans actually taste of ice cream. She also makes dip starters, inspired by the juice bars where she drinks fabulous tropical concoctions. Tonight Hannah makes her Four Mile Beach Guacamole, with basil and lime. I cook the red throat emperor and barramundi and the glorious Australian wine sweetens my dreams.

Fear is a strange beast, or in my case a strange fish. The next day I find myself heading out onto the deep, deep blue, hopefully without a great white in sight. We are part of a 29 tourist group boat today. Vanessa, one of the crew, asks us to stow our shoes in a plastic box on the wooden jetty before boarding. The shoe box is used as a final headcount at the end of the day, to make sure no-one has been left behind on the reef. On board people are helping themselves

to coffee, tea and anti-motion sickness pills. I take two and look through the box of flippers and goggles. I need the flippers that have 'big' painted on them. The skipper jokes that 'big' flippers will help attract the sharks! Jeff and Hannah find this hilarious.

Nearly two hours out and it's wet suit time. Across the ocean we see our first reef submerged like a giant slumbering whale. The water here is fairly shallow, to get us used to snorkelling. I was expecting a safe, enclosed area of reef surrounded by divers looking out for you, or sharks. All I can see is mile upon mile of open exposed ocean, we're supposed to jump in. I'm a tad apprehensive as I sit on the rear-duckboard, goggles and snorkel on, then slide into the Pacific Ocean. The cold hits first but once our heads are beneath the waves everything else is put from my mind, almost. I keep a constant eye out for Hannah and fins. Once underwater the surface above reflects the coral below, like a sky full of trees. Bewildering layers of pattern and colours converge as forms and swirling textures coalesce under the waves. I can't see any fish. A current washes across this chaotic scene like someone turning on a light and all the disparate forms suddenly become separate and whole. Shoals of miniature bright blue fish that had appeared stuck to the coral shift in grouped layers come into sharp focus; larger fish undulate slightly and also become visible. We float, looking down, being swept and swayed in unison with the shoals of fish. Time moves slowly.

Having travelled 9,000 miles to experience this ocean I'm reminded of the fact that the United Nations consider the world's seas and oceans to be the property of the citizens, not governments or fisheries. As well as being a resource for food they're also there for our enjoyment. As with our disappearing rainforests the underwater world is a complex, interconnected web with interdependencies that we have little understanding of. Increasingly the idea of marine reserves are being put forward as a way to halt the damage being done to the oceans. South of here, in New Zealand, are No Take Zones where not only fishing is banned in an area of sea but also any other human intervention such as the extraction of marine aggregate or oil.

Swimming out to the nearby reef we're told to keep an eye out to our left into the deep water in case passing tuna or sharks are lurking. They're likely to be white tip reef sharks, which are rather shy, but we might see larger sharks such as tigers or whalers. Parrot fish weave in and out of the shadows, shoals of thin silver fish shimmer and a blue-rimmed iridescent clam shines like neon in the depths. When in the water the horizon line vanishes, replaced by rising and falling swirls. All we feel is the next wave surging towards us. Away to our left the boat bobs gently. I spit out a salty mouthful, my chin clears the frothy surface. The sky darkens and I feel a sudden stinging on my arms and head. Expecting the worst I look frantically for the translucent tentacles of a box jellyfish, but it's hail stones hitting me and the water around. A fragile and surprising sound, clattering down, as if the water surface were made of marble. The light changes again as we float together on the ocean. Slowly and quietly it begins to rain.

By plunging into these shark-infested waters we've witnessed the dazzling synergy of nature flowing between the humid rainforest of the Daintree to the fish encrusted Great Barrier Reef. Any slithers of ichthyophoia left in me have dissipated, I'm left instead with a growing concern for fish and their habitat and of marine reserves.

AN UNEXPECTED TRIP FOR ART AND
RESEARCH WILL TAKE US TO THE
HEART OF THE SEAFOOD MACHINE
– JAPAN. PERHAPS THE STREETS OF
TOKYO ARE PAVED IN FISH SCALES?

A FISH IN THE MACHINE

TOKYO

ON THE KITCHEN TABLE ARE THREE
AIRLINE TICKETS TO TOKYO, THE
HEART OF THE SEAFOOD WORLD.
AN ART PROJECT ABOUT EELS AND A
CERAMICS EXHIBITION ARE TAKING
THE THREE OF US ACROSS THE GLOBE
TO JAPAN, WHERE 30% OF THE
WORLD'S TUNA AND ONE IN TEN OF
EVERY FISH CAUGHT ARE EATEN.

A red-uniformed check-in assistant at Heathrow asks if I've packed my bag myself.
'Do you claim any responsibility for the ecological impact you'll have on where you're travelling
to today, sir?' she asks, 'There's a twenty per cent discount for anyone possessing an eco-friendly
investment portfolio, entitling you to a ten per cent saving on the airport shuttle bus.
If you take the bus you also get a twenty per cent reduction on your hotel bill and a free tour of
the Museum of Agriculture and Fisheries.' I wake from this daydream and after eleven hours
aboard a cramped jumbo jet we touch down at a cold Narita airport in February.

Tokyo's layered mix of old and new buildings is utterly beguiling. My first introduction to
Tokyo as a child was in 1967, in Panavision, courtesy of the James Bond film *You Only Live Twice*.
By chance I visited the empty volcano film set from the film at Pinewood Studios with a school
friend. We played alone in the flimsy, illusory structures; it was like an apocalyptic playground.
This formative experience inspired me decades later to make sculptural dioramas of typical
south London neighbourhood shops, the backs of which I covered in large hand-painted Japanese
adverts inspired by Ridley Scott's film *Blade Runner*. It was a film that cemented Tokyo as
a 'must-go' destination for me, if only to order a bowl of noodles in a rain-filled street under
faulty, flickering neon. *Blade Runner* beautifully captures the technological infiltration, textures
and linguistic cross-overs of Tokyo, where the contemporary world collides with the old and is
assimilated in a unique way. Although the city in *Blade Runner* is said to be Los Angeles – baring
flashes of the abandoned Bradbury Building and patterned details from Frank Lloyd Wright, the

spirit is all Tokyo, down to the cyclists who appear to have the right-of-way on pavements.

Our passion for neighbourhood shopping has landed us in an old Tokyo *chome* (district) where people still know their mom-and-pop shop owners by name. Staggering, tired, off the Keisei Limited Express at Nippori Station into Yanaka, north-east Tokyo, seeing the cityscape is still a culture shock. My Google Earth satellite map makes the area appear ordered – it couldn't be more misleading. Even in such sharp, radiant February light the level of detail here creates confusion, perhaps it's just sensory overload. We hear a hollow rattling sound, the wind is hitting tall, calligraphy-covered wooden planks leaning against tombstones in the graveyard. Jeff leads us down a narrow twisting alley. At first glance it looks like a back-street flower market. Tight groups of potted plants are piled up against every house facade like riverbanks, making the thin road resemble a meandering dry mountain stream. This vision is in fact how families and shopkeepers extend their houses, not only with flowers but by storing all manner of possessions outdoors. Every millimetre of space is used; hanging brooms, plastic jugs, collapsible chairs, bamboo screens, cooking implements, racks of ladders and pack-away washing lines. Bare trees merge with the organic cluster of overhead wiring radiating across and along the streets like spectral fishing nets.

Yanaka is a typical *shitamachi* district, meaning 'low city'. This pre-war Tokyo housing survived both the Kanto earthquake in 1923 and the fire bombings of the Second World War. The mixture of housing types and small shops is like viewing a large extended family across the generations, old relatives survive in house form (or their era does), slowly melting into the present day vernacular. This glorious mix of architectural styles has a wide palette of materials and a fastidious attention to detail, whether built yesterday or 200 years ago. Idiosyncrasies shine through, grafted together from air-conditioning vents, automatic doors, every electrical appliance you can imagine, dangling oval washing-lines and street signs. An urban collage that has taken centuries to make and whose embellished feel can't be faked. To attune our eyes further we visit the Shitamachi museum in Ueno, and the Tokyo-Edo Tatemono-en museum, an open-air architectural museum of shops and building styles in Koganei Park outside Tokyo.

Returning to Japan after fifteen years is like lifting a veil. I suddenly realise the influence it has had on our lives over that time, seeping into many aspects of our life in London. From drinking delicate green tea, to a garden full of bamboo and carefully placed rocks, to a love of packaging. Not a slavish imitation, more a slow integration. Our front garden is reminiscent of the makeshift collage approach to front gardens we find in Yanaka. A place to store beautiful objects, piled alongside potted plants, logs, crab shells, and bunches of dry bay leaves next to a plastic gas meter box – very backstreet Tokyo.

We spend the days walking the narrow streets, exploring every shop. Hannah and I had made a trial run in central London, browsing through the small Japanese supermarkets. The food packaging was bewildering, often with no visual representation of what's inside the box at all, just huge wandering typography squeezed together with a few cartoon characters. We tried to guess, failing every time. After a week immersed in Yanaka we move to the bright lights and marble-lined boulevards of Ginza to a *ryokan* (inn) named Yoshimizu, within early-morning walking distance of the largest fish market on this blue ocean-covered planet – Tsukiji, the Tokyo Metropolitan Central Wholesale Market.

食品サンプル

FOOD MODELS

SIMMERED MACKEREL

A surprisingly simple way to cook mackerel – blanching and then simmering an oily fish keeps any fishy smells at bay, useful in a small kitchen. This method of cooking is quick and delivers a sweet thick sauce, perfect with a pile of plain rice and some steamed greens. Blanching is used elsewhere in Japanese cookery, with chicken pieces often being blanched to remove fat.

SERVES 3

2 mackerel

175ml water

2 tablespoons sake

1 teaspoon caster sugar

½ teaspoon soy sauce

1 tablespoon mirin

1 teaspoon red miso

1 x 3cm cube ginger, cut into julienne strips (optional)

1 white onion, thinly sliced (optional)

Cut your mackerel into three equal-sized rectangles and make an 'X'-shaped incision on both sides of each piece. Bring a pan of water to boil and place the mackerel fillets in the water. Blanch for two minutes, remove the fillets and plunge them into cold water to cool.

Add the water, sake and sugar to a pan that will fit all the fish in one layer. Bring to a simmer and put in the mackerel pieces and soya sauce. Cover the mackerel with a wooden drop lid or a circle of foil or baking paper. (You'd find wooden drop-lids in most Japanese kitchens, they fit snugly inside a pan on top the ingredients allowing some steam to escape up the sides but not sealing it in.) Simmer gently for 10–15 minutes, turning the fish after 5 minutes. Add the mixture below when you turn the fish.

In a small pan mix the mirin and miso and a few tablespoons of liquid from the mackerel pan. Once the miso has dissolved add it to the mackerel, adding the onion and ginger if you like.

Remove the fish to a warm dish. Simmer the remaining sauce to reduce it. It might require sieving before it's served. Serve with sticky rice and steamed greens.

ATLANTIC MACKEREL
JAPANESE: *Marusaba, hirasaba, saba*
COMMON NAMES: *Mackerel, Boston mackerel, joey*
SPECIES: *Scomber scombrus Linnaeus, 1758*
FAMILY: *Scombridae (Mackerels, Tunas, Bonitos)*

CHUB MACKEREL
JAPANESE: *Hirasaba, honsaba, ma-saba, osabanoko, matsuwasaba, saba*
COMMON NAMES: *Chub mackerel, Pacific mackerel, blue mackerel, hardhead, bullseye, big-eyed mackerel, greenback mackerel, Spanish mackerel*
SPECIES: *Scomber japonicus, Houttuyn, 1782*
FAMILY: *Scombridae (Mackerels, Tunas, Bonitos)*

NORI

JAPANESE: *Nori*
COMMON NAME: *Laver*
SPECIES: *Porphyra yezoensis, ueda; (Porphyra tenera), Kjellman*
FAMILY: *Bangiaceae*

AONORI: Flakes of dried green laver.
MAZE-NORI: Dried red laver mixed with other seaweeds.
AJITSUKE-NORI: Seasoned with soy sauce, mirin and wasabi and re-dried red laver.
IWANORI: Rock seaweed harvested from the shoreline, sold whole and dried.
NAMANORI: Sheets of untoasted *nori* – highly prized and expensive.
FURIKAKE: Bought in bottles – a dry mix of *nori*, sesame seeds and bonito flakes. I even sprinkle it on Chinese takeouts – great on rice or steamed veg too.

SEAWEED 海藻

The Japanese use at least twenty-one species of seaweed in the kitchen, in every conceivable area of cooking. The three main species of edible seaweed are *kombu*, (*Laminaria*), *nori* (*Porphyra*), and *wakame* (*Undaria pinnatifida*).

Kombu

Kombu is an olive-green giant kelp seaweed that is a key ingredient for one of the basics of Japanese cooking, dashi – a stock made from dried bonito and *kombu*. *Kombu* is also eaten in stews and soups, re-hydrated and tied in ribbons.

Wakame

Wakame has green fronds and is usually sold dried for use in soups or salads. When soaked it expands and has a subtle, sweet flavour and is slightly chewy. In soups it only requires simmering for a minute or so. It's also available fresh.

Nori

Nori is perhaps the most visible seaweed in Japanese cuisine as it's used in sushi worldwide. These thin dried seaweed sheets are also used for wrapping rice balls and as a topping or condiment for soups and noodles. Toast briefly before use to reawaken the flavours. The seaweed species used in *nori*, the red alga *Porphyra*, is known as laver in the UK.

NORI POTATO CAKES

1 sheet **nori**, *18 x 20cm*
200g potato, cooked and mashed
1 teaspoon sesame oil
1 tablespoon mirin
1 tablespoon soy sauce
1 tablespoon white sesame seeds, toasted

Cut the nori sheet into seven centimetre squares. Place a small tablespoon of potato on each square.

In a frying pan heat the sesame oil.

Fry the squares potato side down until golden, then turn briefly to fry the *nori* side.

Arrange the fried squares on a dish, *nori* side up.

Mix the mirin and soy sauce and drizzle over the squares.
Garnish with the toasted white sesame seeds.

KYURI TO WAKAME NO SUNOMONO
CUCUMBER SEAWEED SALAD

ワカメ
WAKAME

JAPANESE: *Wakame, ito-wakame, kizami-wakami, nambu wakame, precious sea grass*
COMMON NAMES: *Asian kelp, apron-ribbon vegetable, Japanese kelp*
SPECIES: *Undaria pinnatifida (Harvey) Suringar, 1873*
FAMILY: *Alariaceae*

This delicious wet salad is also used as a condiment and served with rice and fish. It's like an impromptu pickle or relish. Some cooks simmer the *sanbaizu* mixture and let it cool, then add it to the cucumber. The salad will keep in the fridge for a few days.

SERVES 4

2 tablespoons dried wakame
1 cucumber, finely sliced with a mandolin
50ml water
1 teaspoon salt

Sanbaizu
4 tablespoons rice vinegar
1 tablespoon soy sauce
1 tablespoon caster sugar

Put the *wakame* into a bowl of cold water to rehydrate. It will quadruple in size in 10 minutes.

Put the cucumber slices into a bowl. Add the water and salt and leave to stand for 15 minutes.

Drain the cucumber slices then gently squeeze them to remove excess water. Rinse the re-hydrated *wakame* and squeeze out any water. Cut off any hard spines and chop into bite-sized pieces.

To make the *sanbaizu*, in a bowl combine the rice vinegar, soy sauce and sugar until it dissolves. Pour over the cucumber and *wakame*. Refrigerate for an hour or so before eating.

Undaria pinnatifida is listed in the Global Invasive Species Database top 100. It has spread via ship ballast water to France, Great Britain, Spain, Italy, Argentina, Australia, New Zealand, Southern California and San Francisco Bay.

Wakame is processed in different ways:

HOSHI WAKAME: Dried *undaria pinnatifida*.

SARASHI WAKAME: Dried *undaria* after soaking in fresh water.

NARUTO WAKAME: Dried by sprinkling ashes on the surface, washed and re-dried. Often produced in Tokushima Prefecture.

NANBU WAKAME: Harvested in Iwate and Miyagi Prefectures.

伊勢志摩特産

美しい海、伝統の寒摘み。

あおさのり

味噌汁・吸物・天ぷらに…

中央区 佃

キュウリとワカメの酢のもの

SEAWEED ROCKCAKES

IN LONDON I'M A MEMBER OF THE CAKE COMMITTEE – A SMALL GROUP WHO BAKE FOR QUARTERLY TEA PARTIES TO RAISE MONEY FOR LOCAL CHARITIES .

For The Cake Committee, whose motto is: Baking with passion, obsession, madness and art, I wanted to bake something unusual that also involved designing packaging. We had just come back from Tokyo where I had bought a packet of high-quality *wakame*. Seaweed and cakes seemed the perfect pairing.

WAKAME
SEE: *page 166*

MAKES 12 ROCK CAKES

10g wakame	*70g granulated sugar*
110g butter	*1 egg*
225g self-raising flour	*2 tablespoons milk*

Preheat the oven to 190°C/ Gas Mark 5.

Re-hydrate the *wakame* in cold water for 5 minutes. You may have more than you need when re-hydrated, it depends on the *wakame*, you only need about a handful. Cut the re-hydrated *wakame* into small pieces.

Rub butter into the flour in a bowl. Add the sugar and *wakame*. Beat the egg with the milk and add to the cake mixture. Mix together with a fork. Using the fork put rough heaps of the mixture onto a greased oven tray, keeping the heaps well apart as they expand during cooking.

Bake in the preheated oven for about 12 minutes.

Jake TILSON
ワカメ・ロックケーキ
SEAWEED ROCK CAKES

文京区千駄木三丁目
BUNKYO CITY SENDAGI 3-CHOME
44
44-11

The Cake
COMMIT-
TEE

現在地
You are here

ワカメ
ロックケーキ

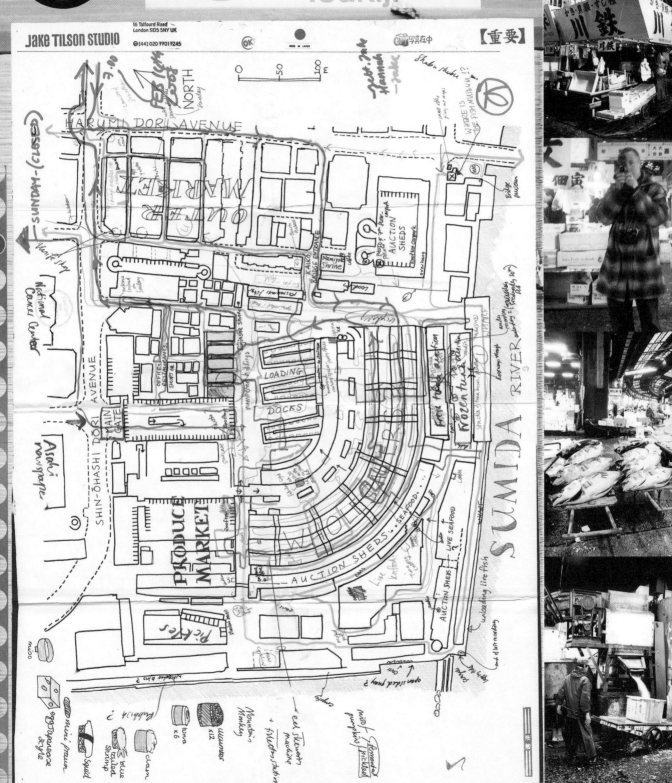

FIRST CONTACT

The Tsukiji fish market was built 73 years ago this month, in February 1935 on reclaimed land from Tokyo Bay. Tsukiji literally means 'built land'. It's not too early, about 5.00am. Slippers on, we descend quickly in the tiny lift to the tranquil lobby. Our street shoes are waiting for us in orderly rows amongst the other guests' footwear. Through gently swaying bamboo I can see the streets are still quiet. Jeff unscrews the sliding door lock, and we all step into a pale, cold Tokyo morning. Winding our way through the deserted streets we cross over a motorway partially covered in park land. Once off the main thoroughfares in Ginza the global architecture slips away and local traits awaken, old wooden buildings nestle in the shadows of tall skyscrapers.

Leaving Ginza we hear, and then see, our first market inhabitant. It appears to be a man carrying a large orange dustbin in front of him, onto which a torch has been strapped, moving incredibly fast towards us. He's actually standing in a motorized three-wheeled flatbed cart, called a *taretto* (turrets). It buzzes and rattles along Shin-Ohasi Dori. The front wheel is hidden behind a rusty metal skirt, making the vehicle appear to hover slightly. He twists the cart sharply by rotating the entire dustbin-shaped engine cover. This solitary drone, separated from the hive, heads off into the empty streets to make a delivery of fish.

The next sign of seafood we encounter is the smell of boiling octopus wafting out of the thin pressed-metal doors of a small side street warehouse. Rectangular wire baskets full of octopus are being lowered into gurgling vats of boiling water, curling their tentacles into a permanent and final flower-like grimace. Further on we detect the sweet smell of *tamago yaki*, sushi omelette, another small firm hard at work in the outer streets.

Nothing quite prepares us for the sight through the main entrance to Tsukiji as we step through the gawping market gates. Walking ahead is treacherous as we dodge the anarchic traffic coming at us from all directions, criss-crossing every inch of slippery, fishy tarmac. We try to divert our attention from the traffic to glimpse the end-view of a long curved railway terminus-like building housing 1,700 wholesale market stalls. Behind this steel edifice are the long wharf-side sheds for auctioning tuna and other live and fresh fish. Jutting out of the wholesale building, like three covered Victorian piers, are the distributors' loading bays with their refrigerated lorries, trucks, vans, motorbikes, scooters, hand carts, bicycles, and many other mechanized vehicles whose species seem strange and new to us as they crash about in the early morning light.

This whole mechanical clanking enterprise is like a sprawling multi-limbed dark and mysterious machine, recently crawled out of the sea and slowly being fed a mountain of Styrofoam by twenty-six thousand workers. The market's pock-marked concrete walls and cobbled alleyways are being washed down with either saltwater or freshwater that is sloshed about as if trying to dowse a volcano. A blackened, archaic apparatus whose exposed cranks move great chains and gears crushes ice into battered chutes. We constantly need to manoeuvre around the workers, the maniacal, vertically driven *taretto* (turrets), buzzing scooters and dangerously quiet two-wheeled wooden handcarts called *neko* (cats). Jeff, Hannah and I step timidly through this torrent of noise into yet another, the bazaar network of wholesale stalls, crammed together in a tight, traffic-snarled grid. And then we suddenly notice the silent fish. They seem almost lost amidst this frenetic activity, like boxes of immaculately packed, exotic gem-stones. It's as if a great wave broke over the banks of the Sumida river this morning, filling the empty sheds and cold halls with glistening fish from every ocean.

We are just three of the 50,000 people who will visit the market today. We cross the entire length of the gently curving cobbled hall, stepping aside to let buyers get past. We look up at

the underside of an intricate metal roof below which are the flat painted stall-signs and finally down at the fish – nearly 1200 species for sale on any day. It seems as if the world's oceans have been scooped up and laid out for us all to see, then buy, cook and eat. The Food and Agriculture Organisation of the United Nations states that the Japanese eat one in ten of every fish caught. An extraordinary figure but one that is sadly believable looking at the fish on sale today. Our local convenience store in Ginza sells a dozen types of packaged seafood snacks such as dried squid and small salted fish, sushi platters and a myriad other seafood dishes. A small Tokyo supermarket will stock perhaps thirty marine species, larger stores fifty – some will be alive and the quality and freshness is breathtaking. Even the language here is fishy, the small triangular-shaped serif-like ends of characters are called *uroko* (fish scales). With a growing understanding of the issues facing a nation that consumes such a huge quantity of fish, I'm relieved to know that The Marine Stewardship Council launched a sustainable seafood labelling system here in 2006. They face a steep climb. There are more than 22 million people in the greater Tokyo area. Let's hope their love for seafood can be harnessed into a concern for its future.If Japanese consumers get behind the MSC scheme it could revolutionise fish production globally.

Refrigerated airfreighting for seafood was pioneered here to supply the market with species from distant oceans to make up the shortfall of the Japanese fishing fleets, which could no longer supply the huge demand for what is perceived as being indigenous. Another demand from the public is that of standardized seafood. In particular the *kata* of a product, it's ideal form, a generic blueprint. Tsujiki merchants need to match this idealized expectation when choosing fish.

As we look about for somewhere to eat I look back over my shoulder, there is much more to explore and to think about, it will have to wait until next week. Jeff and Hannah are finding all sorts of interesting fish-related printed matter littering the ground which they hand to me as impromptu birthday presents. After such a fishy start to the day we find a ceramics supplier for Jeff in Ikebukuro to buy mineral oxides, chosen by their empirical formula, which like scientific fish names have a global language. And then on to a 100yen store for Hannah in Sunshine City, where we all end up buying things. I find a rectangular frying pan to make sushi omelettes and a rectangular grill to cook fish directly over a gas burner. My birthday cake is a *taiyaki*, a sea bream shaped cake filled with sweetened azuki bean paste. Bream are a lucky fish in Japan – a good choice.

ICHIBAN DASHI FIRST STOCK

To create your own immaculately clear soup you need to make your own dashi –
a Japanese fish-seaweed stock. The leftover *kombu* from making dashi can be used to
make a traditional condiment called *Tsukudani* (see below), so nothing is wasted. If you
only need a cupful for a simmered dish you might want to source some instant *dashi*
(*dashi-no-moto*).

MAKES 1 LITRE

1 litre cold water

30g kombu, *giant kelp*

30g dried bonito flakes

Pour the water into a pan, add the *kombu* and simmer gently It must not boil.
Cook until the *kombu* is soft in the middle, about 10 minutes. Once cooked,
remove the *kombu* and set aside.

Sprinkle in the bonito flakes and then remove the pan from the heat.
As the flakes begin to sink, about 30 seconds, the stock is ready to sieve
through cheesecloth (best held in a metal sieve). Keep the bonito flakes.

The resulting stock is *ichiban dashi* (primary dashi) and can be used
in sauces and soups.

Niban dashi

To make *niban dashi* (secondary dashi), add bonito flakes and the *kombu*
that you used in *ichiban dashi* to 1.5 litres of water over a high heat,
uncovered. Just before it boils, reduce the heat slightly and simmer to reduce
the volume by about a third, this might take 20 minutes. Take off the heat
and add 15g of dried bonito flakes. Let them settle and sieve the stock as
before. Use the kombu to make *tsukudani*.

When cool, dashi can be kept in the fridge for a few days.

TSUKUDANI

SERVES 2

30g kombu, *giant kelp, precooked*
and cut into thin slices
(see above)

1 tablespoon soy sauce

1 teaspoon rice vinegar

2 tablespoons mirin

1 tablespoon sugar

1 teaspoon white sesame seeds

Put the *kombu*, soy sauce, vinegar, mirin and sugar into a pan. Simmer over
a medium heat for 15 minutes, until the *kombu* is soft and most of the liquid
has evaporated. Add sesame seeds, transfer to a bowl and refrigerate. Serve
chilled. This recipe can also be made with *nori* but would require less cooking
– about 5 minutes.

BONITO

JAPANESE: *Hongatsuo,
katsuo, katsuwo,
katuwo, magatsuwo,
mandagatsuwo, mandara*
COMMON NAMES:
*Skipjack tuna, ocean
bonito, aku, arctic bonito,
mushmouth, striped tuna,
oceanic skipjack, striped
bellied bonito, victor fish,
watermelon*
SPECIES: *Katsuwonus
pelamis (Linnaeus, 1758)*
FAMILY: *Scombridae
(Mackerels, Tunas, Bonitos)*

KOMBU

JAPANESE: *Makombu,
ebisume, habariko-kombu,
hirome, minmaya-kombu,
moto-kombu, oki-kombu,
powdered kombu, shinori
kombu, uchi-kombu,
umiyama-kombu*
COMMON NAMES: *Kelp,
tangle, sea cabbage,
oarweed, laminaire*
SPECIES: *Saccharina
japonica (Areschoug, 1851)
C.E.Lane, C.Mayes, Druehl
& G.W.Saunders, 2006.
Laminaria japonica
(Areschoug, 1851)*
FAMILY: *Laminariaceae*

*Kombu comes in many
grades and in various
forms in Japan:*

ORI-KOMBU: Stretched,
dried then folded in a
uniform length.
OBORO-KOMBU: soaked in
vinegar, dried and shaved
into long ribbons.
TORORO-KOMBU: Soaked
in vinegar, dried in thin
ribbons or as flakes
KOBUMAKI: A dried tangle
wrapped around a piece
of fish then cooked with
seasonings.
FUNMATSU-KOMBU: Dried
then pulverised.
AOITA-KOMBU: Dipped
in vinegar, boiled in
saltwater and sometimes
dyed blue, then dried.
SU-KOMBU: Soaked in
sweetened vinegar then
dried.

Saccharina japonica is the
main *kombu* species used
but another 8–11 kelp
species are eaten in Japan.

一番だし

特上削	別製削	血合抜
¥2,800/Kg	¥3,200/Kg	¥3,300/Kg

西物キズ節	薩摩腹節	薩摩背節	薩摩亀節	薩摩本節
¥3,200/Kg	¥3,700/Kg	¥4,500/Kg	¥5,000/Kg	¥5,000/Kg

	だしパック	混合厚削	鯖厚削	宗田厚削	鰹厚削
¥750	¥1,450	¥1,700	¥1,900	¥2,300	¥2,700

ハマグリのお吸いもの
CLEAR CLAM SOUP

I've been looking for a way to cook large clams since I had a disaster with a bagful of quahogs in New York when I treated them like small clams. Simmering them in *ichiban dashi* (page 174) results in a delicious, delicate soup. This recipe uses *mitsuba* (trefoil) which is a Japanese wild chervil. *Yuzu* is a Japanese citrus fruit which has a flavour somewhere between lemon and lime.

SERVES 4

12 live hardshell clams, 370g

1 litre ichiban dashi *stock (page 174)*

½ teaspoon soy sauce

small dash of sake

6 2x2cm cubes firm tofu

5 stalks mitsuba *cut into 4cm lengths*

grated or thinly sliced rind yuzu, *lime or lemon*

Clean the clams well, throwing out any that aren't alive. To test if they are alive, tap the shell with a knife. When tapped they should close.

Put the stock in a saucepan and bring to a boil. Turn the heat down and put in the clams. Simmer until the shells open, about 5 minutes or so. Don't overcook them as they become tough.

Add the soy sauce, sake and tofu. Bring back to the boil briefly, then remove from the heat.

Ladle into individual bowls and garnish with the *mitsuba* and *yuzu* rind just before serving.

Variation

Strips of cooked *kombu* tied into bows can be added to this soup. Soak the *kombu* for 15 minutes in cold water to make it pliable. Cut into 15cm long strips, a few centimeters wide, and tie a knot in each strip. These *kombu* bows will need to cook for 30 minutes or so in boiling water before adding to the soup.

NORTHERN QUAHOG
COMMON NAMES: *Hardshell clam, quahog, round clam*
Smallest: *Countnecks*
Medium: *Littlenecks*
Medium-large: *Topnecks*
Large: *Cherrystones*
Largest: *Quahogs or chowder clams*
SPECIES: *Mercenaria mercenaria (Linnaeus, 1758)*
FAMILY: *Veneridae (Venus clams)*

ハマグリ

COMMON ORIENTAL CLAM
COMMON NAMES: *Hardshell clam. quahog, round clam*
SPECIES: *Meretrix lusoria (Roeding, 1798)*
FAMILY: *Veneridae (Venus Clams)*

SOLID SURF CLAM
COMMON NAMES: *Thick trough shell*
SPECIES: *Spisula solida (Linnaeus, 1758)*
FAMILY: *Mactridae (Surf Clams)*

ATLANTIC SURFCLAM
COMMON NAMES: *Bar clam, hen clam*
SPECIES: *Spisula solidissima (Dillwyn, 1817)*
FAMILY: *Mactridae (Surf Clams)*

SERVE YOURSELF SUSHI & SASHIMI

HAND-ROLLED SUSHI, *TEMAKI-ZUSHI*, IS A PERFECT WAY TO CELEBRATE GOOD FRESH FISH: RAW, CURED, SMOKED OR PICKLED.

Arriving at our friends Heechang, Shinano and Aru, on the outskirts of Tokyo, we find that we're all making sushi for lunch. I'm a little worried – sushi always looks rather intimidating, involving bamboo mats. Today though, we're at the easy end of sushi making – *temaki-zushi*, which are little folded squares of nori seaweed filled with rice, vegetables and fish. As easy as making a sandwich. The essential wrapping ingredients are sheets of *nori* seaweed. Also key is the use of Japanese rice with *kombu* stock and rice vinegar, though jasmine rice is a good substitute. The fillings shouldn't follow a slavish sushi-wish-list; use local and seasonal vegetables and fish. If I were making this in Scotland I might use fresh mackerel, salmon roe and some smoked fish – salmon, mackerel or trout. In Venice I'd try Adriatic squid, octopus and crabmeat.

SERVES 4

1 x 28g bag of nori *seaweed* (10 sheets)

Vinegared rice

290ml water

250g Japanese rice

12cm strip of kombu *(dried kelp)*

40ml rice vinegar

1 tablespoon caster sugar

½ teaspoon salt

Fillings

2-egg omelette, sliced into thin strips

200g sushi-quality fresh fish (see above), cut into bite-sized pieces

¼ cucumber, cut into thin strips

2 avocados, cut into thin slices

1 handful small lettuce leaves

wasabi paste (optional)

mayonnaise (optional)

soy sauce (optional)

To make the vinegared rice, wash the rice well, drain and leave to dry for 1 hour.

Put the rice, water and *kombu* into a pan, bring to a boil then remove the *kombu*. Simmer over a moderate heat, covered, for 5 minutes then reduce the heat to as low as possible and continue to cook for a further 15 minutes. Turn up the heat for 5 seconds, remove from the heat. Leave covered.

Add the vinegar, sugar and salt to a small pan, heat gently until dissolved.

Using a flat wooden spoon gently turn the rice into a wooden bowl, fanning it between spoonfuls and slowly add the warm dressing. The aim is to cool the cooked rice whilst gradually adding the vinegared dressing. To keep the rice warm place a damp cloth over the bowl.

Lay out your various fillings on a plate, gather round and start making your own hand-rolled sushi. Place a 12cm square sheet of seaweed in your hand, add a small spoonful of rice in the middle, maybe a smear of wasabi, then some fish, vegetables, omelette and mayonaise – roll into the shape of a cornet, dip a corner into soy sauce, and enjoy.

手巻き寿司

フタを開ける

LIFTING THE LID

A few days later at 6.45am I help Jeff and Hannah pull their luggage along Showa-Dori in Ginza for the airport bus. I'll have to explore the rest of Tsukiji by myself.

Back to Tsukiji. To gain a sense of the scale of such a vast site I start by walking its boundary in the late afternoon when the frantic market traffic has abated, taking in wharf-side views and back alley routes. To try to comprehend the interior space requires a visit when it's empty, so I sneak in late at night. Luckily a large truck blocks my view of the guard-house at the side gate. I walk briskly across moonlit tarmac into the gloom of a loading bay, silent and empty. To avoid a patrolman I slip into the darkness of the wholesale hall. Pitch black and still, the only sound is the steady thrumming of hundreds of padlocked stainless-steel chest-freezers packed with tuna gold, resembling 21st-century mausoleums. Walking alone amongst thousands of stalls the stifling atmosphere is rather disquietening. The hacked, worn butchering blocks are drying out, phones are quiet, tools packed away, invoice books stashed – not a fish in sight. I wander for an hour, getting lost many times. Exiting the hall near the auction sheds I breathe a sigh of relief to be outside and spot my first Tsukiji cat, who darts quickly under a handcart. That night I dream of fish and wake easily at 4am, hopefully in time to catch the tuna auctions.

When contemplating this visit I was tempted to stand outside the tuna auction with a World Wildlife Fund or Greenpeace banner. Maybe I left my conscience at Gate 52 at Heathrow. But this is definitely an observational trip, so like the other gathered tourists I find myself standing in the freezing cold outside a desolate, bunker-like frozen tuna auction shed at 4.30am next to the Sumida River. It's easy to see the fascination that draws people here to this truly bizarre sight, but it's as far removed from a plate of seafood as I can possibly imagine. It is hypocritical to put all the blame of overfishing on the Japanese, even with their large seafood diet. We too have mismanaged one of the world's greatest resources of fish on our own doorsteps.

This surely is the outer ring of hell for bluefin tuna as their majestic carcasses progress from the riverside auction halls, through knives and band saws before adorning small piles of sushi rice. Row upon row of deep frozen tuna resembling embalmed cadavers are being painted with numbers and marks to point out defects. They're also emblazoned with brightly printed pieces of paper, alerting the bidder to where the fish were caught, or farmed, and their weight. Auctioneers from various auction houses stand on sturdy wooden stools, vigorously ringing hand-bells to announce their next auction lot to the bidders. These bidders are examining the tuna with hand-picks and torches, rubbing little pieces of tail flesh between their fingers to determine fat content. The Daito auction house auctioneer points his hand roofwards, dancing and chanting his lots, a fascinating and morbid song. The bidders barely move, except to raise a hand. The whole spectacle resembles an eerie art installation, or the temporary mortuary for a train crash. Some of these tuna are taken by hand-cart to the band-saw shed, like a joiners workshop, until you realise the wood is in fact flesh. Other frozen tuna are wheeled straight into the wholesale area where the huge fresh tuna have also been delivered after their auctions.

Watching a team of four highly-skilled workers dismember a whole tuna is like witnessing a *bunraku* puppet play where a team of puppeteers dressed in black move, manipulate and give life to an inanimate puppet. The care and delicacy with which the four tuna merchants hold, position, cut, wipe and skilfully slice these huge fish is surprisingly touching and ceremonial, and like *bunraku* the team is choreographed by a single master. The sword-shaped knives are five feet long, I can't help but think of samurai. As in Venice and other seafood destinations

local specialities have broken free from their taxonomic confines and developed new culinary categorizations that are all about taste, seasonality, size, maturity and even the location and date on which the fish are caught, all giving the fish product a new name. Some of these factors also make the produce auspicious, an extremely potent and important part of Japanese culture. The fatty *toro* cut of bluefun tuna may seem an immovable gastronomic icon in Japan, but it's relatively new as *toro* used to be the cheapest cut of tuna, fed to cats. Things do change and hopefully they'll shift again before the species becomes extinct.

I spend the next seven days in Tsukiji alone, walking for several hours at a time taking pictures, making notes drawings maps and subsisting on coffee from the outer-ring coffee vending machines that define the periphery of the market zone. A milky sweet mix, 80 yen for a quick fix. I occasionally duck out of the commercial hubbub for a few yakitori skewers in the outer domestic market, or eat a pallid bun from a stall I discover behind one of the ice-suppliers on the inner circuit squeezed between towering wooden fish crates.

On these exploratory walks I wander the outlying edges. I find myself being drawn to architectural details, packaging, stall layout, typography and the intimidating tools of the trade. But a photograph can't sum up the experience of Tsukiji. Its colliding mercantile narratives contain all the passion and intrigue of a Shakespearian tragedy and the convoluted storylines of Dickens. It's an immersive experience, an ancient and almost incoherent environment with few 21st-century trappings except for the traffic and the occasional mobile phone. Not a computer in sight.

Out the back, when the auctions are long finished, the echoing halls are cleared of any remaining detritus – a gold mine to a collage artist. Along the curved bustling thoroughfare I pick over an imaginary high tide mark of rubbish from a thousand shorelines. In the late morning I collect discarded auction tickets stained with fish blood and saltwater, a kindly auctioneer gives me a full clean book, an extraordinarily generous act considering how many tourists plague the market. You have to know what is being cleared away and when, or it soon disappears. The next flotsam to float past into the garbage piles are luminescent shells and printed wooden boxes as the wholesale merchants begin to discard their rubbish. Rummaging around I find elegant almost translucent, fan-tailed shells, arkshells and abalone shells, and a wooden salmon box with bold printed Japanese text. Back at the *ryokan* I wash the tickets and make use of the heated toilet seat, drying them between sheets of newspaper laid across it. The salmon box is slightly too bulky for my case, I wash it in the hotel shower, leaving the door shut to keep in any smell of fish. Thankfully the shower is hermetically sealed. I borrow a hammer from the hotel to disassemble the box into planks so I can take it home.

Back to the market as it winds down. Cleaning crews are hard at work feeding the styrofoam beast and washing everything down, there's not much left by midday. The styrofoam is recycled into blocks on site, for export. As the auction halls become dark and empty I'm reminded of Jeff's love of rusty objects, I find a flattened tin can, which even the Tsukiji cleaners can't pick up off their roads. They might wonder why this February their back roads are looking so free of cans – I have them all, washed and drying on the balcony back at the *ryokan*.

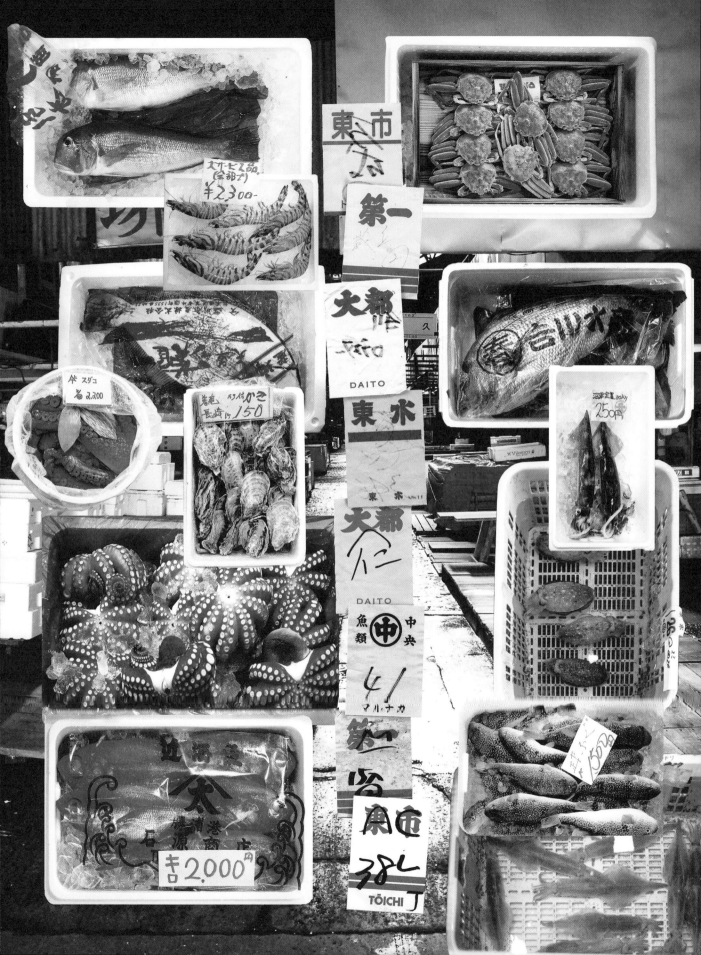

SAIKYO-ZUKE SWEET MISO-MARINATED COLEY

Sweet miso and fish are a match made in heaven. I've cut back slightly on the miso and not added sugar, as some variations on this recipe suggest – the dish is sometimes referred to as fish candy. It goes well with the cucumber and seaweed salad on page 166. Black cod, or bass is often suggested, but I've found coley to be an inexpensive and delicious alternative.
SERVES 3

3 coley fillets, skin on and pin-
    boned
salt (optional)

Marinade
100ml mirin
250g sweet white miso
50ml sake

To make the marinade, bring the mirin to a simmer in a small pan then stir in the white miso and sake. Leave to cool.

Check the fillets for bones and cut each into three same-thickness pieces. This may produce small thin offcuts which can be grilled for less time.

(At this stage Japanese cooks salt their fish, refrigerate them and then rinse off the salt and pat dry. I tend to miss out this step.)

Place the fillets in an air-tight container and pour over the marinade, mix well. Refrigerate for at least 24 hours, or even a few days.

When ready to cook, gently wipe off most of the marinade, leaving a small film.

Grill the fish under a medium heat, not too close, until the skin is crispy and the flesh is moist with sweet, brown edges. If you are using a thicker fillet of fish, such as bass, you can grill the fillets on both sides until the edges brown, then bake in a hot oven until the fish has cooked through.

Heat the remaining marinade in a pan to use as a sauce. Pour over the grilled fillets.

Variation
A Japanese friend, Megumi, recommended replacing half the miso with yoghurt.

西京漬け

ニジマスの焼きもの

にじます

RAINBOW TROUT

JAPANESE: *Niji-masu*
COMMON NAMES: *Steelhead trout, coast angel trout*
SPECIES: *Oncorhynchus mykiss (Walbaum, 1792)*
FAMILY: *Salmonidae (Salmon)*

魚拓

GYOTAKU

From *gyo* 'fish' + *taku* 'rubbing' – a form of Japanese fish printing, dating from the mid 1800s, used by fishermen to record their catches. Some people dry the fish with salt first before applying a waterbased ink – and then taking an impression of the fish.

Yakimono means 'grilled things'. To keep the fillets flat under the fierce heat of a grill I use a Japanese skewering technique called *hira-gushi*, described below, making use of a drawer full of thin bamboo skewers I've had for years and have never known what to do with. The other key to this recipe are the stiff egg whites which add such a delicate texture that I continue to baste during the grilling. This is such a quick dish to make and the method of grilling and basting works well with other fish.

SERVES 3

1 tablespoon salt
2 rainbow trout, filleted, skinned and cut into equal-sized rectangles

1 egg white
1 tablespoon sake
1 tablespoon mirin

Rub salt into the fillet pieces and refrigerate for 2 hours. (This is a particularly Japanese way to season fish.)

Preheat the grill to medium heat.

Wash the salt off the fillet pieces and dry.

Flat skewering, *hira-gushi*. In one hand hold in parallel a pair of thin bamboo skewers about 3 centimetres apart, then push and skewer the fillets. This will help keep the fillet pieces flat.

Whisk the egg white to soft peaks, then gently fold in the sake and mirin. Brush the fillets with this mixture.

Grill for a few minutes each side, turning once. Keep brushing the skewers with the egg white mix whilst cooking.

Serve with plain rice, or on a noodle soup sprinkled with thin strips of *nori* seaweed.

マグロ

LOST AT SEA

海に迷い込む

It's been ten days now. I'm getting further into the bowels of this unstoppable machine. On my last visit to the market I approach the main entrance to be greeted by the words 'Hello Mr Tilson, you're here again'. It's Naoto-san, the friendly ex-salmon auctioneer who took me round the market a few mornings back. As I leave the *ryokan* so early, often the only words I'll speak all day are to the occasional tourist as they ask for directions or advice. Maybe holding a microphone makes me look like a tour guide – I've been recording the sounds of the market. A year later I actually give an impromptu guided tour to a fish buyer from Los Angeles.

At the height of the market's activity it's almost impossible to find somewhere safe to stand. Tsukiji's various spaces are in a constant state of flux. A gently curving hall with numbered columns open on both sides will start the morning as a brightly lit arcade stacked high with fresh seafood, a hubbub of potential buyers inspecting with auctioneers overseeing. After a swift, carefully choreographed ballet of fork lift trucks swirl and whir backwards and sideways at ferocious speed, the same hall is suddenly dark and vacant.

Sculptural makeshift offices are cudgelled together from a mixture of old chairs, weather-beaten telephones and used fish boxes in various states of disrepair, like the remnants of a shipwrecked trawler. Once their job is done these temporary retail spaces are carefully stacked away, each component piled and fitted neatly together like a Swiss army knife.

Around midday I realise I've been walking almost without stop for seven hours. My shoes are stained with a crusty white rim of salt and fish scales. What at first appeared to be a bewildering

bedlam has become embalming and hypnotic, even soothing. As I move deeper and deeper into this habitat I find myself in the catacombs under the spot-lit glare of the wholesalers' stalls with their secretive dead-end storage alleys and makeshift tree-house offices like the medina in Fez. At the centre of this giant, watery cobbled maze of plywood I finally discover the eel-skewering machine which I've been hunting down for days. I also notice small shallow trays of *zotoli*, delicate pinks and purples under the glare of halogen. Going further into this phantasmagorical forest of signs I'm serenaded by the sound of band-saws at work on frozen tuna carcasses and the gentle sploshing and splashing of live fish. Ahead stretches an endless scene like a warehouse of discarded scenery. The edges begin to blur and pale winter sunlight cascades through the dusky skylights high above me, creating a soft glistening glow on the billions of fish scales below. I'm beginning to wonder if I can ever leave.

On all levels the Japanese obsession with seafood has exceeded my wildest dreams, yet it fills my nightmares too. If I had thought the route to extinction for a fish species was to be eaten globally in sandwich bars I was wrong. Sitting atop a piece of sushi rice seems to be a guaranteed deathblow for a species, whether here or in New York, London, Paris, Sydney or Moscow. Yet most seafood dishes in Japan are not wasteful of any part of the fish. Everything is eaten, which as a thrifty cook I greatly admire. Japan is not a gluttonous society. One cannot escape the love Japanese feel for seafood, and their ingenious uses and extensive knowledge of it. *Sashimi* has to be the purest and most respectful form of eating seafood imaginable. It's taught me to treat the seafood that I eat and cook in a similar fashion, with respect. I'm left shattered and exhausted, but also exhilarated. Shaken from any preconceptions about what species of fish I might consider eating. An average supermarket in an outlying Tokyo back street has a wider, fresher range of seafood in better condition than I've seen anywhere other than in Tsukiji itself. Finding anything close in London is going to be a serious challenge. Being here has strengthened my resolve about eating ethically and I'm still finding taxonomy useful. I bought a fish book in Tsukiji full of Linnaeus's influence which listed many of the fish we saw on the Great Barrier Reef and some I saw in New York's Chinatown, all of which are eaten in Japan.

A few months later I find myself sitting in an Italian restaurant in London wondering what my Japanese friend sitting next to me likes on the menu. She smiles, looks me in the eye and says 'fish'. I think many Japanese would rather give up breathing than be denied seafood.

AFTER A WEARY WEEK BACK AT BASE HANNAH IS CALLING ME A JETLAG DRAMA QUEEN. AS I RECOVER I REALISE THAT JAPAN HAS GIVEN ME NEW EYES FOR FISH AND I'VE BECOME COMPLETELY OBSESSED. IN JAPAN, NOWHERE IS MORE THAN 93 MILES FROM THE COAST. IN BRITAIN IT'S ABOUT 70 MILES OR LESS. YET IN SPITE OF THIS, BRITAIN LACKS THE ADVENTUROUS SEAFOOD HABITS OF JAPAN – AS I FIND OUT WHEN RESEARCHING AN ART PROJECT ON EELS.

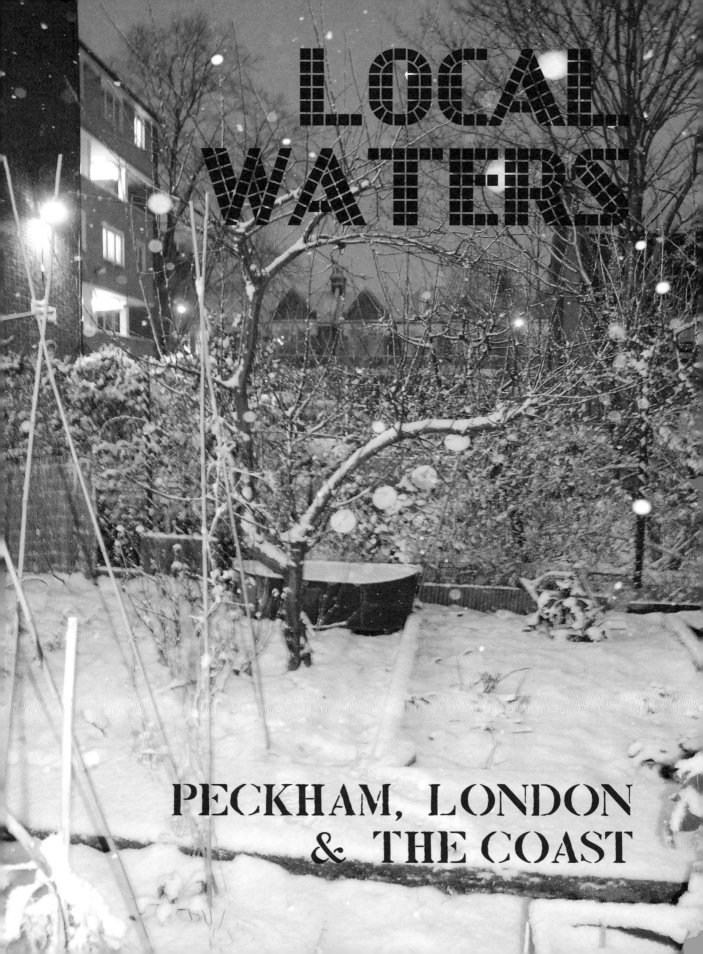

LOCAL WATERS

PECKHAM, LONDON & THE COAST

EVENTUALLY I
MANAGE TO PULL
MYSELF AWAY
FROM THE SIRENS
OF TSUKIJI AND
GET BACK HOME
TO THE GIRLS.

MY SUITCASE
REEKS OF DRIED
FISH AND IS FULL OF MARKET
FRAGMENTS – A LITTLE BIT OF TSUKIJI IN
PECKHAM. HANNAH HAS BEEN EATING WITH CHOPSTICKS
ALL WEEK AND JEFF HAS COOKED DELICIOUS NOODLE SOUP
SPRINKLED WITH DRIED *WAKAME* SEAWEED.
IT'S TIME TO APPLY WHAT I'VE LEARNT ABOUT FISH TO OUR
KITCHEN IN LONDON, BUT THE WORD 'SANCTIMONIOUS', HEARD AT
A CONFERENCE ON FISH, THROWS ME BACK IN AT THE DEEP END.

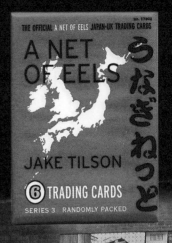

LOOKING LOCAL

SHELL FISH FISH

It's been a few years now since I started this seafood adventure, trying to introduce some culinary marine life into our kitchen in Peckham. Using our work-focused family travels to cure a fear of fish has worked. I've shucked off my fish phobias and have avoided passing on a second-hand phobia to Hannah. As a family we now eat all manner of seafood and our house contains the echoes and traces of shorelines, seas and oceans from across the world. Only yesterday I found a crab shell in my pocket from Watson's Bay in Sydney and I have spent my last two birthdays at the Tsukiji fish market in Tokyo. My studio resembles a nautically-themed pub, draped with fishing nets, buoys, charts, dried squid, clam shells, smoked fish, species posters, canned seafood and the detritus of commercial fish markets. I've slowly become obsessed, not just with eating fish and finding recipes but also with the fate of the fishing towns and villages we've visited along many coastlines, whose history is the sea and whose communities are wholly reliant upon it. But above all I've become fascinated by fish themselves.

On these travels I've purposefully remained a non-professional seafood punter whether observing the high street, markets or dockside. Encountering seafood as a regular shopper reminds me of my recent ignorance on the subject. But working on an art project called *A Net of Eels* – a three year exploration of the complex cultural and culinary significance of the eel in Japan and the UK – changes my mind. Eventually I know too much about eels, including the sad fact that they are critically endangered. I watch as eels enter head-line news status and some eel fisheries close in Europe. As I eat my last eel I realise I am facing a similar dilemma with my new-found love of fish. Many species I want to cook and write about come with a minefield of hidden issues. I scan scientific websites and read hundreds of reports and dozens of books discussing the major issues of overfishing, ocean acidification and pollution, as well as those of: discards, by-catch, beam-trawling, long-lining, fads, ghost fishing, mangrove deforestation, piracy, pesticides, illegal catches, super trawlers, imposex, traceability, aquaculture, parasites, eco labels, biomass, demersal species, pelagic species – the list alone could fill this entire chapter. These issues are

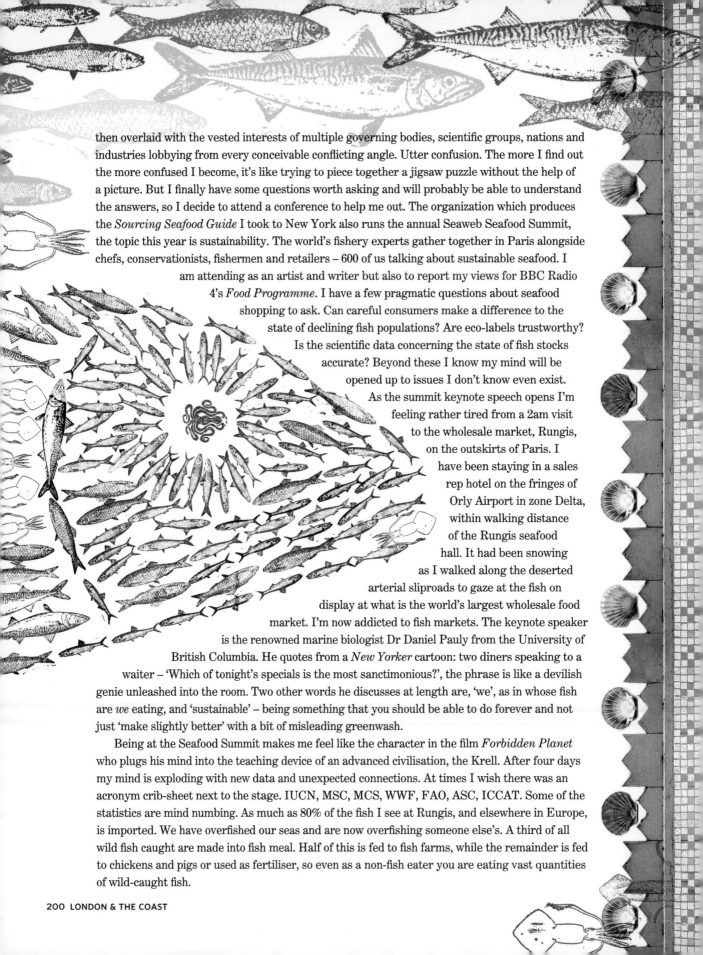

then overlaid with the vested interests of multiple governing bodies, scientific groups, nations and industries lobbying from every conceivable conflicting angle. Utter confusion. The more I find out the more confused I become, it's like trying to piece together a jigsaw puzzle without the help of a picture. But I finally have some questions worth asking and will probably be able to understand the answers, so I decide to attend a conference to help me out. The organization which produces the *Sourcing Seafood Guide* I took to New York also runs the annual Seaweb Seafood Summit, the topic this year is sustainability. The world's fishery experts gather together in Paris alongside chefs, conservationists, fishermen and retailers – 600 of us talking about sustainable seafood. I am attending as an artist and writer but also to report my views for BBC Radio 4's *Food Programme*. I have a few pragmatic questions about seafood shopping to ask. Can careful consumers make a difference to the state of declining fish populations? Are eco-labels trustworthy? Is the scientific data concerning the state of fish stocks accurate? Beyond these I know my mind will be opened up to issues I don't know even exist. As the summit keynote speech opens I'm feeling rather tired from a 2am visit to the wholesale market, Rungis, on the outskirts of Paris. I have been staying in a sales rep hotel on the fringes of Orly Airport in zone Delta, within walking distance of the Rungis seafood hall. It had been snowing as I walked along the deserted arterial sliproads to gaze at the fish on display at what is the world's largest wholesale food market. I'm now addicted to fish markets. The keynote speaker is the renowned marine biologist Dr Daniel Pauly from the University of British Columbia. He quotes from a *New Yorker* cartoon: two diners speaking to a waiter – 'Which of tonight's specials is the most sanctimonious?', the phrase is like a devilish genie unleashed into the room. Two other words he discusses at length are, 'we', as in whose fish are *we* eating, and 'sustainable' – being something that you should be able to do forever and not just 'make slightly better' with a bit of misleading greenwash.

Being at the Seafood Summit makes me feel like the character in the film *Forbidden Planet* who plugs his mind into the teaching device of an advanced civilisation, the Krell. After four days my mind is exploding with new data and unexpected connections. At times I wish there was an acronym crib-sheet next to the stage. IUCN, MSC, MCS, WWF, FAO, ASC, ICCAT. Some of the statistics are mind numbing. As much as 80% of the fish I see at Rungis, and elsewhere in Europe, is imported. We have overfished our seas and are now overfishing someone else's. A third of all wild fish caught are made into fish meal. Half of this is fed to fish farms, while the remainder is fed to chickens and pigs or used as fertiliser, so even as a non-fish eater you are eating vast quantities of wild-caught fish.

Having read so much about the subject it's fascinating to come face to face with the representatives of various organisations as they take to the stage. Hearing them speak first-hand puts into focus what I've read and makes me realise who I can trust. The presentations reveal seriously complex issues, most of which could be dealt with easily as the science to solve overfishing exists, however the political willpower to do so does not. With the failure of governments worldwide another trend is emerging, D.I.Y. conservation. Fishermen who have witnessed the decimation of their fishing grounds find ways to protect them. At another end of the food chain is the exemplary project PISCES, run by Caroline Bennett and Malcolm MacGarvin in the UK. It's a programme designed to help restaurants source sustainable fish by setting up direct contact between chefs and local fishermen. It's a gradual process but one that benefits both sides.

My hotel in Paris overlooks Rue Daguerre, which I first visited 27 years ago. At that time Paris only had one or two Japanese restaurants in the entire city, neither of which served seafood. Today on Rue Daguerre alone there are five sushi restaurants.

Before leaving the summit I have the chance to interview Daniel Pauly – you have to find a voice that you trust. Pauly co-authored the book *In A Perfect Ocean* which reminds me of Alan Davidson's cookbook *North Atlantic Seafood* as both deal with a whole ocean, an entire eco-system. Pauly's book looks at data going back centuries and contrasts past abundance in our oceans with today's beleaguered fish stocks. It provides a startling and lucid view of the effects wrought by the chilling efficiency of today's apparently unstoppable high-tech industrialised fishing fleets. Pauly likens it to the Madoff pyramid scheme – these fleets are taking the capital from our oceans rather than living off the interest. It's an industry where expansion is both sending fleets into foreign seas and down to the seas' depths to find species never before fished. I ask Dr Pauly whether consumers could change the fate of certain species by shopping for seafood with care. Such an approach, he thinks, is at best peripheral and at worst sanctimonious – consumer pressure alone will not be enough, although it is useful to send a message and influence other consumers. To effect real change requires moving up the chain of command, to large-scale buyers of fish and to governments and organisations. As well as not consuming certain species of fish we must lobby governments and give support to protest groups involved in marine conservation and ocean nature reserves.

So what can the ethically minded cook do? Scour the internet each week before shopping? I do three things. First I gradually inform myself about which fish I should be eating or avoiding using seafood consumer guides. These are available as small foldout-sheets or even as updated Apps for your mobile phone. Some guides are better than others, so I consult a Greenpeace or World Wildlife Fund guide from time to time for their unbiased views. Secondly, whenever possible I buy from a source that has been certified as 'sustainable', such as fish labelled with a Marine Stewardship Council logo, although Greenpeace as yet do not endorse the MSC so commonsense should be used. Thirdly, and perhaps most importantly I join groups and campaigns to lobby government to protect our oceans not only by implementing the catch restrictions suggested by scientists but also to support the establishment of more marine reserves. Steps 1 and 2 on their own are not enough, but at last I feel a sense of empowerment that makes me optimistic about eating fish.

:FRIED FISH,WILTED: :HERBS,NOODLES:

KING MACKEREL

COMMON NAMES: *Cavalla, kingfish, hog, kings.*

SPECIES: *Scomberomorus cavalla (Cuvier, 1829)*
FAMILY: *Scombridae (Mackerels, Tunas, Bonitos)*

Trying to cook this dish without ever having seen or eaten it is like approaching a fogbound shoreline. As I attempt my first testing, a week before Hannah and I travel to Venice, the dish begins to take form. I need to be on *Cha ca* street in Hanoi, just to glimpse into one of the many restaurants. Fortunately our visit to Cabramatta, the Vietnamese suburb of Sydney, allowed us to taste spectacular Vietnamese food. In the dishes we ate there I remember deep layers of herbs, and in particular the mint, which lay hidden under the noodles. I suddenly understand *cha ca* – it's about layering – herbs and noodles topped with fish. I can relax. Being a last-minute assembly dish most of the work is done in advance, the actual cooking time is short and won't keep me from our guests too long. The *nuoc cham* sauce helps bring the tastes and colour of the fish to the pale noodles below, creating a vivid orange-red. The fresh mint at the bottom of the bowl is a wonderful surprise. I've since cooked it in Venice for Venetian friends using parsley, red basil and fennel – fabulous.

FINDING THIS RECIPE IN A BOOK BY MADHUR JAFFREY, *FAR EASTERN COOKERY*, I ARM MYSELF WITH SEVERAL VARIATIONS OF THE RECIPE FOUND ONLINE, INCLUDING ONE BY MARK HIX FROM AN EAST LONDON VIETNAMESE RESTAURANT. I WANT TO UNDERSTAND THE BREADTH OF VARIATIONS BEFORE I HAVE A GO MYSELF.

SERVES 4

700g king mackerel steaks, skin removed and cut into 2.5cm cubes

350g rice vermicelli noodles, soaked

2 tablespoons rice flour

1 tablespoon groundnut oil

2 tablespoons finely chopped shallots

3 tablespoons chopped and crushed roasted peanuts

8 spring onions, sliced, greens and whites kept separate

1 large bunch dill, leaves pulled off and stalks discarded

1 large bunch coriander, leaves pulled off and stalks discarded

1 large bunch holy basil, leaves pulled off and stalks discarded

1 bunch mint, leaves pulled off and stalks discarded

nuoc cham *(see page 205)*

Marinade

1 tablespoon groundnut oil

1 tablespoon nuoc mam *Vietnamese fish sauce*

juice of 1 lime

½ teaspoon white wine vinegar

3 cloves garlic, crushed

2 tablespoons finely chopped shallots

1 teaspoon ground turmeric

2 teaspoons galangal powder or grated ginger

Put all the marinade ingredients into a shallow bowl, add the fish and mix well. Cover and leave in the fridge overnight or for a few hours.

In a flat dish soak the noodles in cold water for two hours, or in warm water for 15 minutes.

Bring a large pan of water to boil. Some cooks recommend boiling the noodles in individual portions as they can be difficult to separate when cooked. I tend to cook all the noodles together: put the noodles into the pan, wait for the water to reach a rolling boil again and cook for 1 minute. Check that they are cooked. Rinse under cold running water until cool and leave to drain.

Remove the fish from the fridge. Pour off the marinade. Put the rice flour in a small dish and dust each fish cube lightly in the flour.

Preheat a wok or heavy frying pan, add the groundnut oil and fry the spring onion whites and fish cubes turning gently until cooked, about four minutes. Set aside and keep warm.

Put the shallots and peanuts into the empty wok, cook a few minutes before adding the spring onion greens, dill, coriander and basil. Stir-fry for 30 seconds, wilting the herbs.

Pile the mint leaves into individual serving bowls. Add a small pile of cold cooked noodles and a few tablespoons of the wilted herbs and nuts to each bowl. Top this with a few fried fish cubes and pour over a tablespoon or two of *nuoc cham*.

Have extra *nuoc cham* ready on the table for people to spoon on by themselves. Serve with steamed greens or pak choi.

NƯỚC CHẤM

CHILLI, GARLIC, FISH SAUCE

NUOC MAM

ENGLISH: *Fermented fish sauce*
VIETNAMESE: *Nuoc mam*
CAMBODIAN: *Toeuk trey, tuk trey*
THAI: *Nam bla, nam pla*
BURMESE: *Ngan pya ye, ngan bya yay*
LAOTIAN: *Nam pa*
PHILIPPINES: *Patis*
INDONESIA: *Ketjap ikan*
JAPANESE: *Shottsuru*

Fermented fish sauce, like soy sauce, is used both as a condiment and an ingredient in many South East Asian cuisines in Cambodia, Vietnam, Thailand, Burma, Philippines and even landlocked Laos where the fish sauce is often made from freshwater fish. Usually it's made from anchovies that have been salted and left in water to ferment for up to 12 months and is similar in taste to the ancient Roman fish sauce known as *garum* or *liquamen*. Rather like olive oil there are various grades of fish sauce, so make sure you buy a good one.

A hot, piquant dipping sauce is an essential part of any Vietnamese meal and is a perfect accompaniment to fish dishes such as *cha ca*. I've tried various versions, often using less sugar – in cold Europe I don't feel I need the energy. The key ingredient is a transparent bottled liquid made from fermented fish. The fish used in these bottled sauces changes from country to country along the South China Sea. Experiment with the sauce, adding local and seasonal ingredients of your own. If you develop a taste for fermented fish sauce you can move onto fermented fish paste or shrimp paste.

SERVES 4

4 long red chillies, de-seeded (optional) and finely chopped, plus 1 long red chilli, sliced
3 cloves garlic, crushed
1 tablespoon white wine vinegar
2 tablespoons fresh lime juice
120ml warm water
1 tablespoon caster sugar
2 ½ tablespoons best-quality nuoc mam *Vietnamese fish sauce*

Pound the chopped chillies and garlic in a mortar and pestle into a smooth paste. Put this mixture into a glass jar and add the vinegar, lime juice, water, sugar, fish sauce and sliced chilli. Shake and mix.

Nuoc cham will keep in the fridge and can be made a few days in advance.

TWO-TONE SPRATS

Gold- and copper-coloured sprats – an Autumnal dish using a greatly under-rated fish. It's Guy Fawkes night, November 5th, and we're into the sprat season (October–March). Best eaten using fingers. Sometimes I behead them before frying.

SERVES 4

24 sprats, gutted
rapeseed oil
Spice mix 1
1 teaspoon ground turmeric
1 teaspoon ground ginger
1 teaspoon ground cumin

1 teaspoon ground coriander
salt and pepper
Spice mix 2
4 teaspoons sweet smoked paprika
salt and pepper

Preheat a non-stick frying pan and add a thin layer of rapeseed oil. Mix the spice mixes in two bowls. Dredge half the sprats in Spice mix 1, fry them until golden, about 3 minutes, turning once. Drain the sprats on kitchen paper and wipe the pan. Dredge the remaining sprats in Spice mix 2 and fry as before.

SHORELINE PLATTER

Less of a recipe, perhaps more of an idea. A dish that looks as if it's been washed ashore.

SERVES 4

20 live clams
20 live mussels
2 tablespoons wakame *(see page 166)*
1 glass white wine
8 live razor clams

12 caperberries
1 tablespoon garlic butter
1 red chilli, sliced
2 tablespoons chopped flat-leaf parsley

Scrub the clams, soak for 1 hour in cold water to get rid of any grit. Wash and scrub the mussels, removing any 'beards' that are sticking out and put in a bowl of cold water. Discard any mussels or clams that don't close when tapped. Put the *wakame* into a bowl of cold water for 10 minutes.

Preheat a wide frying pan that has a lid. Chop the *wakame* into strips. Put the *wakame* and mussels into the pan, cook for a minute or so before adding the clams. Put on the lid, cook for 15 seconds, then add the wine. The clams and mussels are cooked when their shells open, which only takes a minute or so. Discard any that don't open.

Brush the razor clam flesh with oil and grill for 3–4 minutes until cooked. Remove the flesh from the shells and cut into slices. Serve alongside the mussels and clams with the caperberries, garlic butter, red chilli and parsley. Accompany with a slab of pre-cooked polenta cut into chip-sized pieces, drizzled with oil and baked in a hot oven for 15 minutes.

When I first began to write and research seafood recipes it seemed important to use a particular fish species as a starting point as they were often crucial to recreating a dish. Eventually I discovered that species identification is probably better suited to marine conservation than for knowing which kind of fish is delicious in a curry. So I began to use recipes for exploration, to try out different ways to cook fish and to help widen my search for local fish wherever we have travelled. I have learnt to find your fish first, then decide how to cook it.

There are many coastal towns within cooking distance of London whose ports supply farmers' markets and restaurants as well as Billingsgate Fish Market, which sits in the shadow of the financial towers of Canary Wharf. Around the coast we visit towns such as Whitstable, Shoreham-on-Sea and Hastings to observe the fishing and to gain a sense of what is landed locally. The fishing fleet at Hastings, whose fishery for herring, mackerel and Dover sole is certified as sustainable by the Marine Stewardship Council, has one of the oldest fishing ports in Britain. A medieval right to use the beach free of charge forever has shaped how the fleet operates. The deep shingle beach, strewn with long fishing nets, crab pots and small rusting bulldozers, is known as the Stade and is home to at least 25 small trawlers. It's the largest beach-launched fleet in Europe. Standing beneath the cliffs on Rock-a-Nore Road are strange buildings that demark the edge of the beach, a surreal cluster of 'net shops'. These black-tarred weatherboard towers rise from small bases like extruded garden sheds, an inviting perch for passing seagulls. On the shoreline a trawler sits beached amongst the lapping waves. Attached to the hull is a steel cable that runs up the beach to a small wooden winch-house, which pulls the boat onshore. Butting up against the many winch houses are weatherboard fresh-fish shacks with flap up fronts revealing ice-covered counters displaying the day's catch for sale. I buy mackerel, huss, flounder and a pair of gurnard and pack them into the cold bag I found at the Sydney Fish Market. Next time I'll bring a lemon, disposable barbecue and a non-stick frying pan and cook on the beach.

In London one of the assumptions I had made before shopping for fish was that my local fishmonger would automatically be displaying detailed labelling about sustainable fish and be sourcing in the same way that a good independent butcher does. I couldn't have been more wrong – it's the large supermarkets who are leading the way with eco-labelling and sourcing, which is probably just as well as they are huge buyers of fish and seem to respond to public pressure. But I still love buying from a fishmonger, I just need to be careful what I chose. In many farmer's markets I've been able to buy directly from small inshore boats, so I can automatically cook what's seasonal and local. From supermarkets we buy MSC-labelled fish: coley, pollack, mackerel or mussels. Discovering how and where a fish was caught is powerful and useful information if you want to know what to avoid.

Loving seafood cookery is as much about mastering the art of what to buy as it is about cooking it. We now eat further down the marine food chain, avoiding the large predators and favouring fast-growing fish that spawn early. We've moved tuna out of sandwich fillings and replaced it with sardines. With the help of which-seafood-to-eat lists I've become familiar with which fish I can eat guilt-free. This knowledge sinks in fast and I can now relax and look for good fresh fish that will taste delicious. I've also joined some lobbying groups such as Greenpeace, Friends of The Earth, and the World Wildlife Fund, as well as a few that advocate the protection of sharks such as the Shark Trust. I've even become a lover of great whites.

MACKEREL KEBABS

Mackerel are a perfect fish for grilling and, when cut into cubes, make seriously delicious kebabs so good that some non-fish eating friends at first thought they were eating lamb.
SERVES 3

4 mackerel fillets, bones removed, cut into 5cm squares

1 red onion, cubed

1 red pepper, sliced

1 courgette cut into 2cm rounds

Marinade

2 teaspoons ground cumin

juice of 1 lemon, plus extra for serving

2 tablespoons olive oil

salt and pepper

Mix the marinade ingredients in a bowl, add the mackerel pieces and vegetables and marinate for an hour.

Preheat the grill to a medium heat.

Skewer the fish, skin side out on 4 skewers, wedged between the vegetable pieces. Brush with some olive oil.

Grill for 5 minutes each side, not too close to the flame, turning to make sure they cook evenly. Squeeze over a little more lemon juice just before serving.

Leftovers

If you have a spare kebab, chop the mackerel and vegetable pieces and wrap in filo pastry. Bake in a preheated oven at 200°C/ Gas Mark 6 for 15 minutes or so.

MACKEREL
SEE: *page* 164

GURNARD & SORREL SAUCE

As well as getting to know seafood over the past few years I've started growing my own fruit, vegetables and herbs in a small allotment across the road. It's wedged between a fire station and a tower-block which stops the sunlight for four months but allows me to do some flood-lit digging if I feel the urge. There's a snowy photograph of it at the beginning of this chapter. My favourite herb crops are the huge amounts of tarragon and sorrel I harvest which I find hard to buy and both of which are made for fish. Gooseberries are on my what-to-plant-for-mackerel list. For this recipe I made this sorrel sauce to go with a pair of gurnard I bought in Hastings straight off a boat within view of the towering net huts.

SERVES 3

GREY GURNARD
COMMON NAMES: *Crooner, gunnard, hardhead, knowd, gowdy*
SPECIES: *Eutrigla gurnardus (Linnaeus, 1758)*
FAMILY: *Triglidae (Searobins)*

2 gurnard, filleted

olive oil

1 tablespoon butter

3 handfuls sorrel leaves, stalks removed

salt and pepper

1 egg yolk (optional)

1 tablespoon double cream (optional)

2 tablespoons crème frâiche (optional)

Melt the butter in a small pan, add the sorrel and cook for a few minutes, stirring. The colour of the sorrel deepens as it cooks. Season with a little salt and pepper.

There are various ways to turn this velvety sorrel puree into a sauce. Some would whisk in an egg yolk and a tablespoon of cream, though just adding a little cream or crème frâiche and heating it through would also work.

Pan fry the gurnard fillets in a little olive oil over a high heat, turning once. They cook quickly, about 3 minutes a side. Serve with the sorrel sauce.

VINE-WRAPPED MACKEREL

It's autumn in London. Jeff has found some windfall apples on the street and our neighbour's vine leaves are creeping over the fence. The glory of this dish is that it gives you an entire fish-shaped-fish with head, tail and skin – but no bones at all – just a sweet stuffing. If you can't get hold of fresh vine leaves, Greek stores sell vine leaves in brine though these will need to be rinsed of salt.

SERVES 3

10 fresh vine leaves, stalks removed

2 whole mackerel, gutted and cleaned

Stuffing

400g apple (sweet), chopped

10 dried pitted apricots, finely chopped

50g breadcrumbs

grated rind of ½ lemon

1 egg yolk

In a wide, shallow pan blanch the fresh vine leaves in boiling water – for about 30 seconds each until they change colour – using tongs.

Cook the apple in a small pan until soft, transfer to a bowl and cool. Add to this the apricots, breadcrumbs and lemon rind, then mix in the egg yolk.

Preheat the to 220°C/ Gas Mark 7.

Prepare the mackerel. The aim is to leave the head and tail intact and remove all of the bones in between – slightly fiddly but worth it. Use a sharp filleting knife. Cut off all the fins, not the tail. Extend the cut along the gutted belly to the tail, cutting up to the backbone. Then without cutting through the flesh and skin, snip through the backbone close to the neck and close to the tail. To help loosen all the bones in between place the fish on a board – belly down with the flaps splayed out. Gently press down on the backbone with your fingers to help release the skeleton from the flesh.

Turn the fish over. You should now be able to remove the backbone and all the attached bones. There are always a few bones left hiding. They can be found with your fingers and removed with pin bone pliers (a must for any fish lover's kitchen).

Stuffing and wrapping the fish will restore its sleek shape. Make a long, overlapping bed of vine leaves that will cover the body of the fish but not the head or tail and place the fish on top.

Put about four tablespoons of stuffing inside each fish. Fold over the vine leaves to restore the shape of the mackerel and hold in the stuffing. Place on an oiled tray.

Bake in the preheated oven for 15 minutes, reduce to 200°C/ Gas Mark 6 and cook a further 20 minutes, or until the fish are cooked.

MACKEREL
SEE: *page 164*

BLUE HORIZONS

Our travels have introduced me to many wonderful ways to cook fish: simmering mackerel in Japan, barbecueing smoked fish in Scotland and infusing an entire dish of Venetian pasta or Vietnamese noodles just using small pieces of intensely flavoured seafood.

Over the past few years immersed in the marine world I'm beginning to get an eye for seasonal fish, so I can look forward to *moeche* in springtime Venice and sprats in autumnal London. I can also navigate the fish section of a Venetian menu with ease and even do it using scientific names; pan-fried *sparus aurata* con Polenta, *pectin jacobaeus* alla Veneziana or perhaps some spaghetti alla *sepiola rondeleti*. With the possibility of genetically engineered farmed salmon I wonder if all farmed fish should be given alternative scientific names? Perhaps I should set up my own classification system, *Salmonidae sapiens* (Tilson, 2011).

I end the story of our ongoing seafood adventure where we started it, in Venice. It's late at night and I'm walking along the wide stone quayside of Fondamenta Zattere with Jeff and Hannah. Mum and Dad are back at the house asleep after another Rialto-bought fish supper. I tried out many new species today, none of which I'd eaten before and some of which the fishmonger only had a handful and didn't know their names – I managed to identify them later. A full moon is rising over the lagoon. Bright streetlights line the edge of Zattere and shine down into the dark water, attracting squid up from the depths. In my hand I have a palm-sized piece of flat cork, a fishing line is coiled around it and on the end dangles a barbed metal shrimp. This device is a squid-lure I bought yesterday in Chioggia, where the Venetian fishing fleet is based. Hundreds of small trawlers are double-parked along the Chioggia canals, sides draped with fishing nets and buoys. My squid lure is almost identical to one we found preserved in the local maritime museum, its design unchanged for centuries, doing the same job today it has always done. Although not for me. There's no luck tonight, just an occasional bite from a ghost-like squid.

As a cook I'm no longer ignorant of the problems facing our oceans, and although there is a shrinking range of fish we should eat, there are enough to keep my culinary inquisitiveness going for decades to come. Not knowing what will appear in our kitchen has been half the fun of cooking seafood. As I explore further I'll continue to abandon myself to experimentation, allowing for disasters and happy to remain slightly lost – it's the only place to be.

READING

Sometimes I found that a single sentence in my book required reading five books, several scientific papers, browsing ten websites and making a visit to another fish market. Here are just some of the more unique or esoteric books I encountered along the way, as a complete list would fill the entire book.

Descrizione de'Pesci, de' Crostacei, e de' Testacei che abitano le Lagune ed il Golfo Veneto, Stefano Chiereghin, 1778-1818. A beautiful facsimile book, a unique historical snapshot of the lagoon. Of the 744 delicate drawings of lagoon species it's interesting to see that most of them are small clams. Quite stunning.

Mediterranean Food, Alan Davidson, Prospect Books, 2002, Penguin Books, 1972. I love this book and take my copy on trips to Italy.

Gondolier's Cook Book: Venetian Traditional Recipes, Marcello Brusegan, Supernova, 1999. A small book, but one I cook from often.

La Cucina Tradizionale Veneta, Dino Coltro, Newton & Compton Editore, 1983. Worth a look if only to view the historic Venetian engravings and culinary illustrations.

La Grande Cucina Veneziana: ricette, storia e cultura della cucina di Venezia, Giampiero Rorato, Daro di Bastiani, 2003. Extensive and authoritative.

A Field Guide to Getting Lost, Rebecca Solnit, Canongate Books, 2006. I stumbled upon a Rececca Solnit quote in a book by Lucy R Lippard whose sources are always worth looking up.

Fishing Across the Centuries: What Prospects for the Venice Lagoon?, S. Silvestri, M Pellizzato and V. Boatto, Nota di Lavoro, 2006. Fascinating.

Gli Animali Commestibili dei mari d'Italia, Arturo Palombi, Mario Santarelli, Hoepli, 1953. Where Davidson may have found a structure for his more extensive book on Mediterranean fish.

Pesca Nella Laguna Venezia, Amministrazione della Provincia di Venezia, 1981. Historic fishing methods described and illustrated.

Multilingual Dictionary of Fish and Fish Products, Organisation for Economic Co-operation and Development, Blackwell Science Ltd, Oxford, 2000. Cross references fish names and products across multiple languages – there is now an online version. I'd like an App, please.

The Great Scandinavian Cook Book: an Encyclopaedia of Domestic Cookery, J Audrey Ellison, George Allen and Unwin, 1966.

The Scots Kitchen: Its Tradition and Lore, F Marian McNeil, Blackie & Sons, 1929. A truly great work packed with detail.

A Year in a Scots Kitchen, Celebrating Summers End To Worshipping its Beginning, Catherine Brown, Neil Wilson Publishing, 2002. Some recipes have multiple versions from different eras, so you can cook with a mixture of ingredients or techniques from 1750 to 2002.

The Christian Watt Papers, David Fraser, Paul Harris Publishing, 1983. The harrowing memoir of the life of a Scottish fisherwoman born in 1833.

Salt in the Blood: Scotland's Fishing Communities Past and Present, James Miller, Canongate, 1999.

Fishing Off the Knuckle: the Fishing Villages of Buchan, David W Summers, Centre for Scottish Studies, 1988.

Trawling: celebrating the industry that transformed Aberdeen and North-East Scotland, Raymond Anderson, The Press & Journal, 2007.

North Atlantic Seafood, Alan Davidson, Prospect Books, 2003, Macmillan, 1979.

In a Perfect Ocean: the State of Fisheries and Ecosystems in the North Atlantic Ocean, Daniel Pauly and Jay Maclean, Island Press, 2003.

The Last Fish Tale: The Fate of the Atlantic and our Disappearing Fisheries, Mark Kurlansky, Jonathan Cape, 2008.

Men's Lives: The Surfmen and Baymen of the South Fork, Peter Matthiessen, Vintage Books, 1986. The history and lives of those who have fished off Long Island from 1633-1986. Deeply evocative with a sharp eye for detail, sometimes I felt I was standing in a Dory myself, waiting for the right wave.

Guide to Sea Fishes of Australia: a Comprehensive Reference for Divers and Fishermen, Rudie H Kuiter, New Holland, 1996. Useful, even though it's not aimed at cooks.

Port of Promise: an Illustrated History of Port Douglas North Queensland, Glenville Pike, Pinevale Publications, 1986. A glimpse of the pioneer days.

Decorative Cast Iron in Australia, E Graeme Robertson, Currey O'Neil, 1984. Australian builders loved Victorian ironwork, in their hands it flourished and took new form covering their cities like a florid carpet.

Tsukiji: The Fish Market at the Center of the World, Theodore C. Bestor, University of California Press, Berkeley, 2004.

A Dictionary of Japanese Food: Ingredients & Culture, Richard Hosking, Prospect Books, 1996.

Japanese Cooking: A Simple Art, Shizuo Tsuji, Kodansha International, 1980. Anyone interested in understanding Japanese food should own this.

Recipes of Japanese Cooking, Yuko Fujuita, Natsume, 2004. I bought this helpful basic book at Narita airport.

The Sushi Economy: Globalization and the Making of a Modern Delicacy, Sasha Issenberg, Gotham Books, 2007.

The Zen of Fish: the Story of Sushi from Samurai to Supermarket, Trevor Corson, HarperCollins, 2007. Required reading for anyone about to step inside a sushi bar.

ONLINE HELP

Certain websites have been essential for this book. Some focus on marine life, others look at ecology and some at seafood. I've put the links online. Visit: www.jaketilson.com/fish

MANUSCRIPT

It's a slow route from piles of paper and external hard drives full of photos to a printed cookbook. For such a long project I have many people to thank along the way. I owe special thanks to the wonderful, welcoming team at Quadrille Books. In particular to Jane O'Shea and Alison Cathie for your belief in the project and my editor Simon Davis. Also thanks at Quadrille to Leonie Kellman and Mark McGinlay and for your enthusiasm. Thank you so much Claudia Roden for the kind words you have said about the book – they mean a great deal to me. I'm indebted to my agent Lizzy Kremer at David Higham Associates for your unwavering support and expert advice. Liz Farelly for persuading me when I was half way through designing the book that it would be a good idea to make the artwork printable in more than one language, which led me to develop the New York Neon typeface. Thank you Michael Mack for support and help during the early phase – it is much appreciated. Thanks also go to Jinny Johnson for your support.

EDITING

It was an absolute delight to work with Simon Davis at Quadrille, his eagle eyes and sympathetic approach to my text have restored my faith in editing. For those of you who think 'this recipe is easy to follow' – you have Simon to thank. Before the text

reached Simon there are other people to thank – in particular Jeff, for her meticulous pre-editing, and also Lizzy Kremer who did an invaluable job at a crucial stage.

TRANSLATION

Many thanks to Megumi Yamashita for kindly helping with the Japanese text before I irreversibly stencilled it onto the artwork. Thank you Gabriella Cardazzo for correcting my Italian/Venetian recipe titles before I rubber stamped them. And to Erik Nissen Johansen for your Swedish fishballs assistance. If there are any errors, they're all mine.

ON THE ROAD

In Venice thank you Mario and Assunta di Martino and their late wife and mother Daniela, with whom I would have loved to have spent more time discovering Venetian food. Thanks to Enzo di Martino and Mariella, and also our Venetian neighbours Maria and Ennio for local culinary help and a supply of mussels and other delicacies they fish out of the Adriatic. Our local restaurant Furatola in Calle Lunga San Barnaba and to friends who visited Venice, in particular Simon and Abigail Weinstock, Bruce and Georgia Johnson – all of who let me see Venice through new eyes. In Scotland special thanks go to Andrew and Ruth Ruck for a wonderful fishing trip and barbecue – and to my extended Scottish family: Susie, Bill, Phillipa and Grant Robson, Ernie Lee and Patricia Milligan. In New York massive thanks to Susan Shopmaker and Chris McCann, my gastronomic outpost in Queens. Thanks also to James Oseland, Dana Bowen and Todd Coleman at *Saveur*. Devon Fredericks and Eli Zabar for being culinary icons. Stephen Farthing and Ami Abou-baka, Carole Lalli, Nina Lalli, Susan Friedman, Ann Bramson, Naomi Duguid, Betsy Smith and Dick Smith. At *Food & Wine*; Tina Ujlaki, Salma Abdelnour and Jen Murphy – for all your support and help. In Australia thanks go to Elizabeth Hastings, Sarah Hetherington, Fiona Fraser, Juliet Gauchat and John Cott – and online blog help from Deborah Rodrigo and also from Joanna Savil. Trips to Japan need phenomenal amounts of planning, advice and help. Very special thanks to Issey Miyake, Hiroshi Kamio, Ritsu Yoshino and Piera Berardi. The great Japanese designers Masuteru Aoba and Mitsuo Katsui. Heechang, Shinano and Aru Yoon for being such perfect hosts and showing us how to make *temaki-zushi*. Also the understanding staff at the Yoshimizu Ryokan. I'm indebted to Junko Suwa and Mariko Yagi, Kyoichi Tsuzuki. Some pre-Tsukiji thanks to Nigel Sherman and our dear friend Howard Bern. And thanks to Peter Begg and David Loftus who both persuaded me that I should take a film camera with me to Tsukiji – not just digital. Back in the UK, love and thanks to my sisters Anna and Sophy, and to Rosie, Poppy, Sam, Bill and Albert, and to Paul Scotcher. Thanks to the Oxford Symposium on Food and Cookery for being a place of gastronomic refuge and support.

SEAFOOD HELP

Thank you so much Nancy Harmon Jenkins for speaking about the tricky subject of fish – once via a satellite link from Maine with the help of BBC Radio 4. Thank you Ken Watmough for giving me a personal tour of the Aberdeen fish market, I greatly appreciate your kindness and patience. Seaweb came to the rescue when I had some seafood questions with their Seafood Summit, in Paris – thank you so much Melanie Siggs, Julia Roberson and Valerie Craig. At the summit I interviewed several specialists. In particular I would like to thank Dr Daniel Pauly for sharing his knowledge, wisdom and time. Also Caroline Bennett (Moshi Moshi), and Malcolm MacGarvin with whom I had an extended and inspiring conversation about seafood and the summit. It was a joy to talk to Julie Packard from the Monterey Bay Aquarium and also to Jill Schwartz from the World Wildlife Fund. My visit to the Rungis market was helped by Anyes Estay (MSC Paris) and Philippe STISI (Rungis). Marc Dachy gave me an invaluable lesson in how to pronounce the word Rungis! It was such a pleasure and an honour to work with the BBC Radio 4's *Food Programme* making *Jake's Sustainable Fish*. Huge thanks to the wonderful BBC team; Rebecca Moore, Sheila Dillon, Dan Saladino and Susan Fleming.

EXHIBITIONS

I've had two outings for fish-related artworks so far. In 2009, *A Net of Eels: Jake Tilson & Kyoichi Tsuzuki* was commissioned by The Film and Video Umbrella in London, see page 198. Enormous thanks to Steven Bode, Mike Jones, Nina Ernst and the team at FVU for their supreme professionalism and for what turned out to be such an enjoyable and extended collaboration. *A Net of Eels* was supported by Arts Council England, The Jerwood Charitable Foundation, The Great Britain Sasakawa Foundation and Japan Foundation. It was exhibited at the Wapping Project in London, a spectacular venue – very special thanks to Jules and Josh Wright at Wapping for their energy and vision. The exhibition also toured to the Babylon Gallery in Ely, thanks to Digby Chacksfield. In 2010 I exhibited a tuna related work, *20:1 Bluefin Tuna*, at the *Anti Design Festival* in London (see page 200). The image was made up of hundreds of small fish which had been rubber stamped in the shape of a life-size bluefin on a vertical cloth banner. Special thanks to Neville Brody and Andy Chen for inviting me. To produce a single kilo of ranched (farmed) tuna requires feeding them twenty kilos of edible fish, such as mackerel, herring, sardine, anchovy and squid.

ACKNOWLEDGE-MENTS

There's always much to thank Tom Jaine for. As well as letting me reproduce a page from Alan Davidson's seminal book *Mediterranean Seafood* he introduced me to Richard Hosking who in turn recommended the great book on Japanese food by Shizuo Tsuji. Thanks to the Macduff Aquarium for letting me reproduce my haddock adoption certificate, and to Julie Packard at the Monterey Bay Aquarium for allowing me to reproduce the cover of their excellent *Seafood Watch Guide*.

The author has endeavored to trace all copyright holders and clear rights in connection with photographs and other illustrations reproduced in this book. Not all could be located. Please contact the author at contact@jaketilson.com to notify rights not acknowledged and the publishers will be happy to correct any omission in future editions. This book has in no way been endorsed by any of the brand owners featured in it.

PHOTOGRAPHY

I took all of the photographs except for the various portraits of me, these were kindly taken by: Jennifer (Jeff) Lee p15, p32, p37, p47, p78, p83, p134, p154, p214. Hannah Tilson p68, p161, p169. Andrew Ruck p81. Joe Tilson p6. Adam Levy p108

Warning: All photographs are 100% natural – no styling involved. Every plateful was eaten seconds after being photographed – sometimes before. All crockery was used as-is and as-found, lighting was used as-available. Shot on a 35mm Nikon FM2, Nikon D200, Sony Cyber-shot P120, Canon S90, iPhone4, Super cine8, video8 and videoHi8.

TYPOGRAPHY

I've designed several of the typefaces especially for this book. Each typeface reflects a particular aspect of the location of the chapter.

VENETIAN MARINE

2008. This typeface is based on the stencils found on Venetian boats. For the recipe titles it was then made into a rubber stamp alphabet. Titles were rubber stamped onto paper and scanned for the book.

SCOTTISH FISHERY

2009. Inspired by registration numbers hand-painted on Scottish fishing boats. Each boat has a number of 1, 2 or 3 letters preceding a number – such as BF104 for Banff.

NEW YORK NEON

2008-09. Inspired by the culinary neon signs of New York using photographs taken over several years. To achieve the full neon effect the font has been designed to be used as a fifth colour to be printed over a bright, multi coloured background.

SYDNEY LACE

2008-09. This typeface takes its form from the intricate and beautiful decorative cast ironwork that adorns many Federation era houses in Australia. I took photographs mainly in Sydney and made the typeface from drawings and scans.

NIZIOLETO

2003. This typeface is taken from Venetian street name signage which are stencilled directly onto buildings within a white painted rectangle. For a fuller account of this typeface see the book *3 Found Fonts*, Jake Tilson, Atlas, 2003. An accompanying CD contains three fonts, including nizioleto.